D1130975

UNDERGROUND:

**four plays by
Edgar White**

WILLIAM MORROW AND COMPANY, INC.

New York   1970

UNDERGROUND

four plays by
EDGAR WHITE

FOREWORD

The dramatic style of Edgar White will strike you initially as both familiar and strange—always the sign that you are in the presence of genuine talent. As you reread his work or see it performed by a cast that is right, you will begin to sense something beyond obvious talent, a finally elusive individuality. Edgar White has plenty of skill to make the evening's entertainment move and build. The characters are solidly there and alive. But each play has another kind of interest. Each play as a whole outdistances the most comprehensive voice it contains. There is a context beyond vicariously shared experience. Finally, Edgar White comes through as a writer playfully growing with his language.

Two of the plays in this volume, *The Mummer's Play* and *The Wonderfull Yeare*, I have seen performed at the New York Shakespeare Festival Public Theater. I put that fact on record here to emphasize that Edgar White has conquered the physical reality of theater. His plays make absorbing reading, but they also come alive when played. Audiences must be overcome and these plays can do just that. When I saw them performed I made a careful check of the people in the house. They were definitely what you would call mixed: in age, ethos and life style. They were also cool and needed to be shown. But by the end of the evening we were all together within the action of the play. The artifice had worked the way artifice should, by disappearing.

The titles of these plays suggest how far they can go beyond the purely local action. But don't let that put you off. Everybody wants to meet people who exist clearly in some time and place, who speak first for themselves and who can make themselves felt. Edgar White's people are like that. They speak to you out of graspable situations and places. They belong simply to themselves. But like all real individuals they are unaware of their universality. Only the writer and the good reader know about that.

A few words of guidance. The most sophisticated of these plays is *Fun in Lethe*. This play is what you might call the poetry of allusion. You will catch enough of the tag lines and phrases woven into this Wasteland panorama not to let the hidden ones bother you. The accent has to be on *Fun*. Let the people come on in their own—or what they think is their own—style. Take it all the way Hamartia does. Ride with it.

Perhaps the play with the largest range of focus is *The Burghers of Calais*. Here the writer is closest to his fellow victims but also ready to place them in the broadest stream of the human race. The theatrical perspective is also complex. The play as a play within the play brings us closer to an awareness of life itself as theater. This is a daring venture: tragedy as epic farce.

The Mummer's Play speaks for itself. It comes straight at you like a song.

The allusion in *The Wonderfull Yeare* is to London's deliverance from a plague, among other impending disasters. But even while plagues rage the living have a way of ignoring them. This deeply ironic play is about the gift of life in the midst of death.

There are some writers who are good because they struggle visibly with themselves and their language. Edgar White is good because he is a free man. He defines himself as he works his material, and he draws strength from all the secret and open mines of the English language, past and present.

Richard Harrier
FORMER CHAIRMAN
DEPARTMENT OF ENGLISH
WASHINGTON SQUARE COLLEGE

CONTENTS

THE
BURGHERS
OF CALAIS

DRAMATIS PERSONAE

(In order of appearance)

SIX COUPLES, *visitors to the prison*
THE SPEAKER
THE AUTHOR
A NEWSBOY
TWO BEGGARS
LEADER OF THE COMMUNIST PARTY
FIVE MEMBERS OF THE COMMUNIST PARTY
ELDERLY NEGRO WOMAN *(to be played by the same actress*
                          as the Mother)
TWO LIGHT-SKINNED NEGROES
NAACP LEADER
BROTHER WHITE ⎱
BROTHER JOHNSON ⎰ *NAACP members*
THE SHERIFF (Sheriff Club Hawk)

             BAGATELLE ⎫
             NICKNACK ⎪
                QUID ⎪   *The nine Negro men*
             PRO QUO ⎬ *accused of rape*
     THREE SAD FELLOWS ⎪
TWO SENT TO JUVENILE PRISON ⎭
DEPUTY CORMORANT
LAWYER LEIBY
MISS ELLEN TWITROMP
JUDGE PUDIC
PROSECUTOR
JURY
JOHN DAY, *NAACP member*
MINISTER LAZARILLO

SUSAN DOCILE

THE MOTHER, *Bella Donna*

A HIGH PUBLIC OFFICIAL (of ejaculatio praecox birth—to
be played by the audience not
an actor)

BANQUET HOST, *in Socialist Meeting Hall*

SOCIALISTS AT BANQUET

FOUR NEGROES

ACT ONE
SCENE ONE

[*The drug prison in Lexington, Kentucky. The inmates are putting on the play at teatime for their amusement.*]

SPEAKER. [*He is a black man, wearing shades.*] Ladies, gentlemen, and fellow inmates, we are happy tonight to present to you teatime at Lexington. We will have a jazz recital and a performance of *The Burghers of Calais*. We are fortunate, here at Lexington, to have an abundance of talent. Moreover, to number among our institution certain former judges and lawyers, who have by mischance fallen to certain excesses. [*He laughs mockingly.*] It is the author's intention, wherever possible, to have the actors play themselves. I hope that you find the entertainment at least diverting. This is the story of the Scottsboro Boys, which took place in 1931 and lasted until 1950. I believe the author wrote the story with love. And now the jazz recital.

[*The jazz recital takes place.*]

SCENE TWO

The SPEAKER *returns followed by the* AUTHOR. *The* AUTHOR *is a sullen young Negro who also wears shades. His clothing consists of a black corduroy jacket, an open-collared white shirt, dark trousers and an open scarf. He smokes a pipe. The* AUTHOR *seats himself with back to audience.*]

SPEAKER. I shall now try to give the ethos of the period and perhaps a setting for the drama.

[*He walks about.*]

At the turn of the century America was filled with a certain optimism. The twentieth century would surely bring to fruition the blessings of the industrial revolution. There would be no more poverty, ignorance or superstition. America was on the move. It had survived a hideous and internecine war between North and South. Even the Negro was on his way to democracy and several Negro universities were thriving, thanks to northern philanthropists. America had a vigorous president in Franklin

Roosevelt. Uncle Sam had a virile body. But the depression did a lot to castrate the grand figure which the First World War had produced. By the 30's the Negro had become a tremulous ghost breathing heavily from the back of busses and from beneath certain beds.

[*The* SPEAKER *opens a large book.*]

The New York Times records, 1930. "Negros: *see* Ku Klux Klan, Lynching, and Music." [*He closes book.*] One hot, boring and oppressive summer day, in the hot, boring and oppressive year of our Lord 1931, two girls, Ellen Twitromp and Susan Docile, hoboed their way to Alabama. Accompanying them were six white boys. Also in the train was a group of Negro men. On the way several of the white boys became involved in a game of pushing the Negroes off the train. The Negroes responded by pushing the white boys off the train.

[*Someone laughs.*]

The white boys that were thrown off walked to the nearest town and circulated a story of brutality and rape. A wire was sent to the first station the train stopped at. The marshall of the town, Scottsboro, took the Negroes that he could catch into custody. Nine were apprehended, charged with rape, beaten, and given a speedy trial. The news of this trial reached New York.
The scene is in front of the Communist Party headquarters at Union Square.

NEWSBOY.   [*crying out*] Read all about it, read all about it. Scottsboro boys found guilty of rape.

[*Two* BEGGARS *on a cart crisscross each other on stage. They have no legs.*]

BEGGARS.   [*crying*] Give a few pennies, give a few pennies.

[*Four* ACTORS *come out on stage. They form two couples and join their upraised hand to form a pyramid to symbolize an entranceway, as in a child's game. The* MEMBERS *of the Communist Party are* SIX MEN, *dressed in baggy blue suits and plaid shirts and ties. They are about to go beneath the upraised hands of the* ACTORS *to enter the meeting house when the* AUTHOR *suddenly motions for attention. They stop, the* SPEAKER *comes over to the* AUTHOR *who whispers in his ear.*]

SPEAKER.   The Author says that the sun was shining.

[*An elderly* NEGRO WOMAN *dressed in a maid's outfit comes out onstage, holding a cardboard cutout of the sun. She stands on stage and holds sun up. The* SPEAKER *nods approval. The* MEMBERS *then enter the Communist Hall. They sit at a long table, the* LEADER *at the head.*]

LEADER.   All right, gentlemen, we will now have a reading of the minutes.

MEMBERS.   To hell with all that, Steve, we all know why we're here.

LEADER.   All right then, we'll get right down to the issues. Things are pretty bad right now for us. We've just about lost all the support that we've had. Russia, the Promised Land, is looking goddamn lousy these days. The papers are making a lot of hay about the totalitarian system over there, rumors of executions and what have you. Of course, they don't seem to care too much about what Germany is up to and what this guy Hitler is talking about, but anyway . . . where was I?

MEMBER.   You were about to talk about the Scottsboro boys.

LEADER. Oh . . . yes, brothers, we have an opportunity now to get ourselves some much needed publicity. Not only in our own papers but even in *The New York Times*. These nine boys are pretty hot stuff. If we can get the Negroes to see that we're out to help them we can get something happening with the Party again. We all know how important the Negro is——

MEMBER. How important is he?

LEADER. Damn important to us.

MEMBER. Oh.

LEADER. Here's a chance for us to raise our treasury and our prestige almost threefold.

MEMBER. What should our strategy be?

LEADER. First of all we have to get those boys the best possible lawyer in New York.

MEMBER. Who?

LEADER. Lawyer Leiby.

MEMBER. You know how he hates us. That stupid bastard thinks he's some sort of aristocrat or something.

LEADER. He can be bought if we tickle his ego enough.

MEMBER. Better appeal to his wallet rather than his ego.

LEADER. No, his ego. He doesn't really need the money, he's the most sought after attorney in New York. He can name his price anywhere.

MEMBER. Clever son-of-a-gun, he's never lost a case, has he?

LEADER. I think he lost one, but he hasn't lost since. So that, gentlemen, is the first step.

MEMBER. Suppose he won't join.

LEADER. Then we'll have to get someone else, won't we? As a matter of fact, I've already started arrangements to get that Unitarian minister, Dr. Lazarillo, to come in too, he's a great liberal.

MEMBER. Yeah, but he's not a communist.

LEADER. So much the better. He's so caught up in his American fantasy that he'll fit right in. Liberals are interchangeable.

[*They laugh.*]

SCENE THREE

SPEAKER. Meanwhile at the NAACP headquarters . . .

[*Two light-skinned* NEGROES *well-attired in suits come on stage and repeat the form of the entranceway. Four similarly attired* NEGROES *enter through them.*]

NAACP LEADER. [*He speaks in the droning voice of a Southern gentleman.*] Brothers, the situation is a grave one. Several of our people have been unfairly tried in Alabama. I believe this will prove to be an important trial. I believe we must enter it. Yes, brother White?

BROTHER WHITE. Mr. Chairman, I too have felt the pain of the circumstance. I too know that generations hence shall remember with . . .

NAACP LEADER. Please, brother White, cut the rhetoric and come to your point.

BROTHER WHITE. Yes, well, we simply do not have the strength at this time to become involved in this case.

BROTHER JOHNSON. Mr. Chairman.

NAACP LEADER. Yes, brother Johnson.

BROTHER JOHNSON. Mr. Chairman, I think that it is imperative that we realize that we have no choice in the matter. If we do not act the Party surely will. We have been waiting, and waiting, and if we wait any longer we will be totally ineffective. We must march on until victory is won, not, Mr. Chairman, because we are brazen, but because we have no choice.

LEADER. Well said, brother Johnson.

BROTHER WHITE. Mr. Chairman, speaking realistically, I think the best approach is for one of us to first, go down to Alabama and appraise the situation fully, to find out exactly what our strength might be and, secondly, to find out whether or not these nine boys really did rape those two women.

NAACP LEADER. All right, brother White, one thing is for certain. We have to have some concrete strategy before we act, otherwise we could cause not only our own destruction but serious repercussion on all of our Negro brothers.

SCENE FOUR

[The prison at Scottsboro. The NEGROES *are in a large cage. There is a sign in front of it saying:* Please don't feed the Niggers. *All of the characters wear signs hanging from their necks saying:* I am Negro, *or,* I am white. *On stage is a large white man who is the* SHERIFF.]

SPEAKER. The scene is the prison at Scottsboro. This cellblock has been condemned for white prisoners. Will you open the cage, please?

*[*SHERIFF *opens cage. Nine* NEGROES *come out.]*

These are the Nine.

[They parade around for audience. Seven of them are connected by chains, the other two look on as though confused. The AUTHOR *signals the* SPEAKER, *he whispers to him.]*

Yes, fine. You two on the end may go. They were thirteen and fourteen years of age respectively and therefore were sent to juvenile prison. There, that leaves seven, the perfect number for *The Burghers of Calais.* All right, fellows, carry on.

[The seven NEGROES *begin to do a Greek dance for about five minutes.]*

Yes now, Sheriff Club Hawk, will you, please, relate to us exactly what happened on that day. Firstly with what you were wearing at the time.

SHERIFF. What I was wearing at the time?

SPEAKER. Yes.

SHERIFF. Just what I'm wearing now, corduroy trousers, work shirt, and combat boots.

SPEAKER. Are those the boots you kicked the boys with?

SHERIFF. I didn't kick all of them. Just that one, Bagatelle.

[BAGATELLE *smiles and makes his feet pigeon-toed.*]

He's an uppity nigger, that one.

SPEAKER. What exactly did you do when you took them off the train?

SHERIFF. Well, it went like this: I got them to the station, a lynch mob gathered outside, I questioned the boys.

[*He goes over to the* BOYS.]

This one's name is Bagatelle; this one is Nicknack and these two brothers are Quid and Pro Quo. I asked Nicknack: Did you criminally molest Miss Twitromp?

NICKNACK. What?

BAGATELLE. He means did you fuck her?

NICKNACK. No, I ain't never done that to nobody.

BAGATELLE. He's telling the truth, he ain't never screwed nobody. He once made it with a cow on the farm, and I think he said with a chicken once, too.

NICKNACK. You ain't got to tell him all a that; you don't have to put my damn business in the street.

SHERIFF. You niggers sure are something. Anything that's got a hole, eh? O.K., what about you, Bagatelle?

BAGATELLE. I didn't even see them funny-ass girls. And if I wanted some white trim I could of bought it.

SHERIFF. And what about you two, Quid and Pro Quo, I suppose you all didn't see them either, eh?

QUID. Not me.

PRO QUO. I gots bad eyes.

SHERIFF. Oh yeah, well, they ain't going to get much badder, nigger. I'm going to explain to you all just once. This here is a confession. Now it took my deputy here, Deputy Cormorant, a long time to type it up.

[DEPUTY CORMORANT *comes on stage.*]

DEPUTY CORMORANT. Sure did.

SHERIFF. Now, if you people don't hurry up and sign this . . .

BAGATELLE. I ain't signing my name to nothing.

SHERIFF. Still talking, ah, Bagatelle? Well, if you people don't hurry up and sign I'm going out to have me a large dinner. Now I got me a good healthy appetite and it's probably going to take me a couple of hours to eat. Now my deputy here will probably want to get himself a breath of fresh air sometime soon. Now, you all see that mob out there?

NICKNACK.   What mob?

> [SHERIFF *makes as if opening door;* VOICES *are heard off stage.*]

VOICES.   Kill the niggers! Cut off their black dicks! Teach them a lesson!

SHERIFF.   That mob.

NICKNACK.   Oh, that mob. Where's the pen?

SHERIFF.   I see you get the point.

> [*turns to audience*]

So they signed. The trial was pretty quick. The court assigned them some lawyer, they were found guilty and we were all getting set for the hanging, when I receive this here telegram from Montgomery. "Big New York Lawyer coming to Scottsboro. Lots of newsmen too, clean up prison and prisoners." So, I did.

SPEAKER.   Thank you, Sheriff, that will be all.

> [SHERIFF *is given a red cape by his* DEPUTY *which he puts on and exits stage.*]

Which one is Bagatelle?

BAGATELLE.   That's me.

SPEAKER.   Bagatelle, Nicknack, Quid and Pro Quo and who are the other three?

THE THREE.   We are the three sad fellows. We don't get to speak.

SPEAKER.   Oh all right. Bagatelle, go on.

BAGATELLE.   Well, stupid here commence to panic.

NICKNACK.   I ain't stupid.

BAGATELLE.   Yes you are, you forget?

NICKNACK.   Oh yeah, I forgot. I'm stupid.

BAGATELLE.   Yeah! So, he starts crying and pissing on himself and what not.

NICKNACK.   Oh Lord, I ain't done nothing wrong, why they going to hang me?

BAGATELLE.   You were born black, weren't you? That's what the hell you did wrong.

NICKNACK.   I ain't done nothing but made it with a cow.

BAGATELLE.   You unnatural fellow, you. Well, anyway the next day this lawyer comes storming in.

[VOICE *is heard offstage*]

VOICE.   Where's my negroes?

BAGATELLE.   Oh Lord, I think we going to have some trouble with this cat.

VOICE.   Where are the Scottsboro boys?

BAGATELLE.   We not receiving today, we're on vacation. Anyway he comes in to our cell.

[*enter* LEIBY]

All nice and shiny. He got on a white suit and holding a black briefcase in his hands with his initials on it. He's bald as a marble, and got his nose up in the air like he's smelling something bad.

LEIBY. Hello boys, keep a stout heart, I've come to save you. My name is Attorney Leiby. I've been commissioned to take on your case by the International Labor Defense.

BAGATELLE. How they know about us?

LEIBY. Everyone knows about you, you're all famous.

NICKNACK. You hear that, Bagatelle, I'm famous. Goddamn!

BAGATELLE. Yeah, you're famous, so you going to be dead soon.

LEIBY. Not if I can help it. I'm not in the habit of losing cases.

NICKNACK. Please, Mr. Leiby, do something for me? I don't want to be hung.

BAGATELLE. They wouldn't hang you. They would put you in the electric chair.

NICKNACK. Does that hurt?

BAGATELLE. Not for long.

ACT TWO
SCENE ONE

SPEAKER. The scene is the new trial in Morgan County. A week before, the Governor of California, James Ralph, had congratulated the citizens of San Jose for lynching two Negroes. The entire state of Alabama is a fortress outside of which America is filled with a blond absence of substance. The prosecutrix, Miss Ellen Twitromp, appears early.

[TWITROMP *comes out on stage, kisses the* AUTHOR *gently and seats herself on witness stand.*]

She is attired in a white chiffon dress purchased at J. C. Penney, for two dollars and ninety-eight cents. She is thin and her face is unusually fatigued. This is for three reasons. First, she has over the past several months been haunted by certain nightmares, wherein she finds herself in a darkened room filled with deflated balloons. And there, also in the room, is an old woman with varicose veins. Second, she is fatigued because the trial is taking place on the end of the month and she is having her period.

[*There is a gasp heard from the audience of on-lookers. A* WOMAN *gets up and turns to her husband.*]

WOMAN. Come on, Fred, we don't have to hear anymore.

[*they exit*]

SPEAKER. [*continues*] Third, she is fatigued because she knows everything she has said and everything that she is about to say is a lie. She wears a white straw hat with a long ribbon of a bright and brutal yellow. Despite everything she has beautiful brown eyes.

The Judge, Pudic, is a round, red-faced fellow, with plump hands which he rests on his belly. He looks like a seneschalesque figure in his dark robe. The pleats seem like waves when he walks. He suffers from gout and an unfortunate ailment of the throat which does not permit him to raise his voice above a whisper. His wife, Prudence, has just fed him a lunch of yams, johnie-cakes and chicken fried in . . .

WOMEN IN AUDIENCE. What difference does it make what he ate for lunch? Why all these digressions?

SPEAKER. The Author believes that what a man eats determines the way he sees the world, madam.

[WOMAN *gets up and leaves with* HUSBAND.]

The Attorney for the prosecution is unimportant. He is misshapen and stutters excitedly.

Go on.

PROSECUTOR   Miss Twitromp, sorry to put you through all this again.

TWITROMP.   Oh, it's all right.

PROSECUTOR.   That's a very pretty hat you're wearing.

TWITROMP.   That's very kind of you.

PROSECUTOR.   Miss Twitromp, will you tell us what happened after the niggers kicked the white boys off the train.

TWITROMP.   Well, after the niggers kicked the white boys off the train . . .

LEIBY.   Your honor, I object.

JUDGE.   You ain't got nothing to object to yet.

PROSECUTOR.   Go on, please.

TWITROMP.   Well, the big one there, Bagatelle, he come over to me and he says . . . he says white girl he says . . . I want to eat your salty pussy. White girl!

PROSECUTOR.   I want to eat your salty pussy. Is that what he said?

TWITROMP.   Yes.

PROSECUTOR.   And what did you say?

TWITROMP. I said, get away from me, you dreadful Negro, you.

PROSECUTOR. Then what?

TWITROMP. Then he says, I'm going put something inside you so big that an eagle will be able to make a nest there and that afterwards I'd be able to sing like a black woman. I don't know whatever made him think I'd want to sing like a black woman.

PROSECUTOR. Did he threaten you with anything?

TWITROMP. Yeah! He put this knife to my throat.

PROSECUTOR. So you had no choice, Miss Twitromp, as these brutal, vicious men attacked you.

TWITROMP. Right sir, I was ravished. [*sobs*]

PROSECUTOR. That will be all, Miss Twitromp, very sorry to put you through all this. Your witness, Leiby.

[LEIBY *springs up and stalks her as if she were an animal.*]

LEIBY. So you were attacked, Miss Twitromp.

TWITROMP. Yes, your honor, they forced open my legs and pulled up my skirt.

LEIBY. But you weren't wearing a dress. You and your friend were wearing dungarees at the time.

TWITROMP. Oh! Yes, your honor. I disremembered. I was wearing pants. They pulled them off me.

LEIBY. You don't have to call me your honor, I'm only a simple lawyer.

TWITROMP. Yes, simple lawyer, sir.

[*The court laughs.*]

LEIBY. How old are you, Miss Twitromp?

TWITROMP. I don't rightly know, sir. I ain't too well-educated.

LEIBY. You don't know how old you are?

TWITROMP. No, sir.

LEIBY. Where are you employed?

TWITROMP. I work at the mill, your honor.

LEIBY. Miss Twitromp, it is putatively held that you . . .

TWITROMP. It's what, sir?

LEIBY. It's commonly known that you have done a great deal of prostitution to supplement your income.

TWITROMP. That's a goddamn lie.

PROSECUTOR. I object, your honor.

JUDGE. Objection [*belch*] sustained, the moral character of this witness is not on trial here.

LEIBY. Is it not a fact that you were violating the state law by entering Alabama with several men illegally?

PROSECUTOR. I object, your honor. We are not going . . . going to be led astray by no Jew lawyer from New York who was sent down here with commie money.

SPEAKER. The jury chanted in clarion voice:

JURY. Kill the niggers.

LEIBY. Where I ask you, is your friend, Susan Docile? Why has she been abducted?

TWITROMP. Why don't you ask her that yourself? It was you all who took her.

LEIBY. No further questions. Oh, I'm sorry, one more question. What kind of a knife did Bagatelle have?

TWITROMP. I don't know, it was a big old thing.

LEIBY. Strange that no one has found it.

SHERIFF. [*still wearing cape*] Here you are, your honor. Here's the knife.

LEIBY. Why wasn't this entered as evidence if this was the knife.

SHERIFF. Just clean forgot it, guess I must be getting old.

SPEAKER. The summation for the prosecution was very brief.

PROSECUTOR. Now listen up, you all. I don't want to be taking up your time, or wasting mine. If you people want niggers raping your mothers, wifes, and daughters, you find them innocent, otherwise guilty is the only verdict you can reach. That's all. [*sits*]

LEIBY. Your honor, and members of the jury, never before have I seen such dereliction of justice. Never before has the animalistic cruelty of prejudice been so expressed to me. My clients and even myself have been threatened with lynching. As for myself, I can only say I am not at all afraid. I know this life to be merely a changing form, a mode in a constant universe. I am certain that none of you will comprehend with what equanimity I shall meet my God. I wonder, however, how it's possible for any of you to so flagrantly defy morality. You all know well that these boys are innocent.

A. The reputation of Miss Twitromp is well known to you all. The boys could easily enough have purchased whatever they desired, if they desired.

B. The doctor's report was that there was no finding of violence or sexual molestation to the girls. Of course, also to be considered is the fact that the doctor refuses to give testimony.

C. The young white boy did testify that Bagatelle saved him when he was falling off the train.

D. The disappearance of Susan Docile, the second party in this accused rape, has not been explained.

I plead with you not to bring ignominy to the name of Scottsboro. This will last forever. And lastly I ask for a mistrial on the grounds that the constitution has been violated, as no Negroes were allowed on the jury. I thank you.

SCENE TWO

SPEAKER. The deliberation lasted twenty-six hours. Bagatelle was found guilty and sentenced to death for the second time. Bagatelle rose when he heard the sentence and said:

[BAGATELLE *stands with spotlight on him. He reads as though reciting at school.*]

BAGATELLE. Um . . . in God . . . there is hope.

SCENE THREE

[BAGATELLE *and* NICKNACK]

NICKNACK. They done found your ass guilty again, eh?

BAGATELLE. [*facing other way*] Umm.

NICKNACK. Well, Leiby tried.

BAGATELLE. Yeah, that's just wonderful.

NICKNACK. Bagatelle.

BAGATELLE. What?

NICKNACK. What's it like to make it with a girl.

BAGATELLE. Well it depends, my boy.

NICKNACK. Depends on what?

BAGATELLE. Well now, if you riding some girl who's good, it can be fun. If she's good you don't have to love her. It's sort of like riding a fast mare, everything moves just right. Now when you love, you see, when you love somebody a lot, it's about a hundred times as good. If you got a bad back then you forget you got a bad back. If you got any aches and pains you don't remember them. It's like you diving into the ocean and at the same time leaping into the sky. At the time you believe anything. You believe life's perfect. You believe God's up there smiling for you. Then when you come you just be seeing colors, blazing lights getting duller. You don't know which one of you are crying. Then you find out that really both of you are crying. Now you see, that's love.

NICKNACK.   Wowie! Good God! I gots to get out of here and get into some of that.

SCENE FOUR

[A MEMBER *of the NAACP visits the prison. He has a question mark hanging from his neck, he is neither black nor white.*]

NAACP MAN.   Are you Mr. Bagatelle?

BAGATELLE.   Yeah, that's me.

NAACP MAN.   I'm John Day of the NAACP

BAGATELLE.   Oh, wonderful.

NAACP MAN.   We have been following your case very carefully.

BAGATELLE.   Yeah, me too.

NAACP MAN.   We had to be cautious before we acted. A lot of other people could have gotten needlessly hurt if we hadn't.

BAGATELLE. Oh, a lot of people, eh? You got any cigarettes?

NAACP MAN. Yes, here you are. Here's a lighter.

BAGATELLE. Thanks. I'll just hold on to these. You're free, you can buy some more.

NAACP MAN. Well, I . . .

BAGATELLE. Now about a lot of people being hurt. I was thinking about that as I looked out there at that mob stringing up ropes for us. Weren't we thinking about a lot of people being hurt, Nicknack?

NICKNACK. Yeah, that's just what I was a thinking about, a lot of people being hurt.

BAGATELLE. And you know what I decided. I decided that all Negroes got to get hurt so that they know they niggers. If they all got hit upside their heads, dragged out of beds at midnight, then they'd be ready. Reality is real good, cause then you not confused, you don't have to waste time thinking. Do you understand what I'm saying?

NAACP MAN. I understand. You're very bitter.

BAGATELLE. You see, when a white man gets scared he goes crazy, you understand. There ain't nothing in this world like a scared white man. I mean he'll go out there and kill up everybody else in the country if he gets scared enough. [*pause*]

And he don't ask if you wearing a suit, understand now?

NAACP MAN. I understand. Do you know that the Party has your mothers convinced that we're out to kill you?

NICKNACK. What Party?

BAGATELLE. The Communist Party, stupid.

NAACP MAN. They've even gone so far as to send your mother to Europe, Nicknack, to raise money.

BAGATELLE. She probably just sitting over there running her mouth as usual.

NAACP MAN. As a matter of fact, it's been so successful that they have four women impersonating her at the same time.

NICKNACK. Oh yeah, I got a million mothers, eh?

BAGATELLE. Maybe you got a million fathers too.

NICKNACK. You getting a little too damn cute. Don't be playing the dozens with me or I'm gone have to come over there and rearrange your face. Sorry, Mr. Day, go on.

NAACP MAN. Well, that's all I wanted you to know. That we're definitely not your enemy.

BAGATELLE. You ain't too much of a friend either.

NAACP MAN. We're doing the best we can.

BAGATELLE. Yeah, but that ain't very much.

NAACP MAN. You're right, forgive us. If there is anything at all that we can do though, we will. [takes BAGATELLE's hand] Good-bye, brothers.

[exits]

NICKNACK. Damn, my mother's in Europe. Sure wish I was in Europe.

BAGATELLE. I wish I was anyplace . . . [*pause*] else.

[*Enter* LEIBY *accompanied by Minister* LAZA-RILLO.]

LEIBY. Hello, Scottsboro boys.

BAGATELLE. Hi Leiby, got any cigarettes?

LEIBY. [*giving him pack of cigarettes*] That's all you ever ask for.

BAGATELLE. I'd ask for a shotgun if I thought I could get it.

LEIBY. Here, I even got a present for you—two cigars.

BAGATELLE. Hot damn, just like I was civilized.

LEIBY. Boys, this is Dr. Lazarillo. He's . . . well, why don't you explain, Lazarillo?

LAZARILLO. Hello, guys. I was sent down to assist Mr. Leiby in this case.

LEIBY. I don't need any assistance. I've always been quite capable of handling myself.

LAZARILLO. That may well be, Mr. Leiby, however, in this instance I think you show a singular lack of awareness of the situation here in the South.

LEIBY. If you mean these stupid red-necked bigots, you're right.

LAZARILLO. Yes, that's another thing. I think it did not at all aid your case when you announced that to the press last week.

LEIBY. I've lost my patience with these terrorists. They have no reason.

LAZARILLO. Well, you came down here filled with the certainty that you could move any jury anywhere to see the situation in a clear light. You didn't stop to take into consideration the fact that what was on trial here was not nine boys, but all the accumulated prejudice and fear of the entire South.

LEIBY. All right, if you can do better go ahead. You don't need me.

[LEIBY *storms away.*]

LAZARILLO. He's a very vain person, but I think we can reach him.

BAGATELLE. What do you plan to do?

LAZARILLO. Well, for the appeal we'll have to get a lawyer from the South, familiar with the situations here, and the judges. We can't win by fighting against brick walls. We have to try to win them over to our side.

BAGATELLE. The Communist Party wants us for martyrs to win them popularity. The NAACP and Leiby are interested in the Fourteenth Amendment. What are you interested in?

LAZARILLO. Well, it sounds funny to say it, I guess. I'm interested in justice.

BAGATELLE. Well, I never been too well-acquainted with justice.

LAZARILLO. Yes, I know. I'll promise you one thing though, I'll never stop trying until all of you are out of here. If I don't die.

NICKNACK. You mean if we don't die.

SCENE FIVE

SPEAKER.   The Author would like Susan Docile to appear now.

[SUSAN DOCILE *enters, kisses* AUTHOR *and walks to center of stage. She wears a plain black dress.*]

She is a plain-looking girl and has nothing special to recommend her. She has full lips though, good for chewing on.

[*The* AUTHOR *signals the* SPEAKER.]

Something else?
Oh yes, she's had a difficult life. Miss Docile, please.

DOCILE.   I had to confess. I couldn't stand it anymore. I didn't mean nobody any kind of harm. Ellen said if I didn't say what she said they'd put us in jail and everything. They didn't do anything to us. We didn't even talk to those Negroes.

My mother was never very nice to me. [*turns to* AUTHOR] Can I say that?

SPEAKER.   You can say that.

DOCILE.   Ain't nobody been very nice to me, really, 'cept for Ellen. We been friends a long time. I knew her before she got married the first time. We used to like to walk along the river together, sit and talk and everything. She's really a nice girl, too. Once when I needed some money terrible bad, she stole some for me. A friend is somebody who would steal for you. But I don't want those boys to die on my account. Because it would bother me. I got enough things on my mind anyway.

[*pause*] I once had a baby and—and I . . .

[AUTHOR *signals.*]

SPEAKER. Don't tell us about that.

DOCILE. After I confess I want to go to Chicago. I don't like the South no more. [*pause*] That's all.

[*exit*]

SPEAKER. The Minister Lazarillo's midnight prayer.

[LAZARILLO *in center stage*]

LAZARILLO. Oh, glory-father, we have now come unto a dark wood. My soul is afflicted with doubt, my self is an awkward thing. I have seen men punished without cause, and the guilty flourishing everywhere before me. Help me walk with a certain calm before these my tormentors. Fill me with a careful sleep that I might marvel at thy wonder at my ease. Take me away from the confines of this dull and public world to a place of some certainty. Help me in this my disbelief. Let me not follow a crazed horn like the others. Amen.

SCENE SIX

[BAGATELLE *and the others confront the* AUTHOR.]

BAGATELLE. I'd like to ask the Author a few questions myself.

SPEAKER. Yes?

BAGATELLE. Not you, the Author. [*goes over to* AUTHOR] Why are we trapped here in this drug prison, wasting our lives away? Why are we so trapped? And why is the Author himself here, a drug addict?

[*The* AUTHOR *signals the* SPEAKER.]

SPEAKER. [*after listening to* AUTHOR] The Author feels that a pause would not be amiss here.

[*The* AUTHOR *stands and begins to walk offstage with hands pocketed. One of the female members of the audience throws a flower down to him. He picks it up and walks offstage.*]

ACT THREE
SCENE ONE

[*The scene reopens with the reentrance of the* AUTHOR. *Again there is a confrontation with the* ACTORS. *This time* NICKNACK *takes the lead.*]

NICKNACK. All I want to know is, why does he get to play Bagatelle. I'm a hell of a better actor than he is any day. All I am is a foil for him. He don't look so threatening, I'm taller than he is and got more spirit.

BAGATELLE. Now wait a minute, I can outshine you in any goddamn . . .

[*The* AUTHOR *signals* SPEAKER.]

SPEAKER. The Author says that he couldn't care less if you all killed each other one second after the play is over but now you're interfering with his sense of the aesthetic. Please, take your places.

[*They reluctantly take their places.*]

And now a few words about the genealogy of Bagatelle. Bagatelle's father was a day laborer, and showed some proficiency on the potter's wheel. He was kicked by a mule one day in Georgia.

BAGATELLE. Right in the gut. Died two days after.

SPEAKER. His grandfather, Blackamoor Bagatelle, was a disillusioned Manichean. Enough about that. Bagatelle's Mother's name is Bella Donna. We see her now one spring afternoon in the third year of Bagatelle's imprisonment. She is talking with the Minister Lazarillo. The grass beneath their feet is doing wiggly things from the wind.

[*The* MOTHER *is played by the same elderly* WOMAN *who put the sun in the sky at the opening of the play.*]

LAZARILLO. Mrs. Bella Donna, I know how you feel.

MOTHER. Do you have a son in prison?

LAZARILLO. No.

MOTHER. Have you ever been in prison?

LAZARILLO. No.

MOTHER. Then you don't have no damn idea how I feel.

LAZARILLO. My parents died when I was very young. I grew up with my grandmother. She had a very cruel face, but the softest hands in the world. I'd touch them and fall asleep. You remind me a lot of her.

MOTHER. My hands ain't soft.

LAZARILLO. Mrs. Bella Donna, you've got to trust me.

MOTHER. No, I don't.

LAZARILLO. I'm doing all that I can for your son and the others. We all are.

MOTHER. I've been hearing lies all my life, lies everywhere, from everybody. Lies in the morning, lies in the evening, eat-and-sleep lies.

[*The* AUTHOR *signals.*]

SPEAKER. The Author says he doesn't want to hear anymore of that, it displeases him.

[MOTHER *and* LAZARILLO *and another* COUPLE *from the audience exit.* BAGATELLE *and* NICKNACK *come onstage,* BAGATELLE *watches audience leave, he is smoking a cigar.*]

NICKNACK. Well, they gone give you another trial next week, Bagatelle.

BAGATELLE. So they say.

NICKNACK. What did you tell those newspapermen this morning?

BAGATELLE. I didn't tell them a goddamn thing. They want to know what I'm thinking, let them pay. If I ever get out of here I'm going to sell my story for a lot of money. And I mean a lot.

NICKNACK. You don't think they gone kill you, eh?

BAGATELLE. No, I think there's too much concern now for them to do that.

NICKNACK. Well, you ought to be nicer to Leiby and Dr. Lazarillo. They the ones keeping you alive with all those appeals.

BAGATELLE. Nicer! Listen coconut-head, it's white women who lied and put my ass in this place, it's white people who are keeping me here for a crime I ain't had shit to do with, you understand. I'm not about to be nice to anybody. These people don't know what an evil nigger is yet.

NICKNACK. But they gone learn, eh?

BAGATELLE. They gone learn.

NICKNACK. What are you gone do with the money, if you get it?

BAGATELLE. What am I gone do? I'm going to New York, get myself a castle.

NICKNACK. They got castles in New York?

BAGATELLE. I'm gone make one. Get myself a shopping bag full of cocaine.

NICKNACK. Wo Wee!

BAGATELLE. You understand. I'm going to have a giant smile on my face like Santa Claus. Sit up there with some big-legged women, talking about [*mimicks female voice*] "Do you want anything, Mr. Bagatelle?" No woman, just sit here for a couple hours and let me smell you.

NICKNACK. Yeah!

BAGATELLE. Let her keep my glasses filled and roll my reefers for me.

NICKNACK. I sure hope you make it, man. [*pause*] Hell! I hope I make it. I wish I could read and write.

BAGATELLE. I could teach you whatever I know.

NICKNACK. Would you?

BAGATELLE. Yeah, sure, why not? Lazarillo brought some newspapers and some magazines we can start on these. Here we go: Important German Jew says that reports of Hitler's a-trocity to Jews are all false. Says Hitler is a very sensible leader.

NICKNACK. What's a-trocity, Bagatelle?

BAGATELLE. I don't know, it's not important, anyway. Here's a picture of Rockerfeller being given a gift of flowers by a little girl.

NICKNACK. Let me see.

BAGATELLE. Rockerfeller is the one in the wheelchair.

NICKNACK. Well now, there's only two of them in the picture, did you think I'd of thought Rockerfeller was the little girl?

BAGATELLE. Well, I don't know how you think. I'll teach you to read tomorrow, I'm tired now. Hey, Cormorant, what time is it?

CORMORANT. [*entering stage chewing tobacco*] Same time it was yesterday. What damn difference does it make to you what time it is, you ain't going nowhere.

BAGATELLE. Hey Nicknack, when I leave this place remind me to bash his head in, will you?

NICKNACK. Sure enough, Bagatelle.

CORMORANT. You gone bash whose head in?

BAGATELLE. Yours, you honky bastard.

CORMORANT. [*gets his club and starts at* BAGATELLE] I'll teach you something, nigger.

[*enter* LAZARILLO *and* LEIBY]

LAZARILLO. Hope I'm not interrupting anything, gentlemen.

CORMORANT. That salty nigger's gone get himself killed, believe you me.

BAGATELLE. By gosh, by gingo, by gum.

LEIBY. Could you excuse us a moment, Deputy Cormorant? I would like to speak with my clients.

[CORMORANT *steps out.*]

LAZARILLO. A most unkind fellow.

BAGATELLE. Yeah, a bastard too.

LAZARILLO. Well, I think we might make it this time. Susan
        Docile changed her story, the townspeople are far more
        sympathetic to us now. I think we'll be able to call a
        mistrial on insufficient evidence. What do you say, Leiby?

LEIBY. I don't know for certain whether we'll get ourselves a
        total acquittal, but our chances are certainly better this
        time.

LAZARILLO. Nobody loses all the time.

SCENE TWO

[*The meeting of* BAGATELLE *and the* GRAND INQUIS-
ITOR]

INQUISITOR. Your name is Bagatelle?

BAGATELLE. Yes, sir.

INQUISITOR. You were born of the unfortunate class?

BAGATELLE. Yes, sir.

INQUISITOR. Was there any joy in your having?

BAGATELLE. I wouldn't know, sir.

INQUISITOR. I mean do you remember your mother being happy
        to see you when you were born?

BAGATELLE. I just don't remember, sir.

INQUISITOR.   Yes, of course, he doesn't remember. Tell me, Mr. Bagatelle, wasn't one of your relatives a Carthaginian?

BAGATELLE.   Not that I know of.

INQUISITOR.   [*reading from book*] It says right here, a general from Carthage.

BAGATELLE.   Nope, no relative of mine.

INQUISITOR.   All right, all right, never mind, we'll get back to that later. Now then, where did you learn to read?

BAGATELLE.   I don't know, around I guess?

INQUISITOR.   Um hmm. Around, eh? You ever read Duns Scotus?

BAGATELLE.   No.

INQUISITOR.   Avicenna or St. Thomas Aquinas?

BAGATELLE.   No, I ain't even heard of them.

INQUISITOR.   How about Boethius or St. Anselm?

BAGATELLE.   No, none of them.

INQUISITOR.   Bagatelle, [*pause*] why is God unique?

BAGATELLE.   I don't know; because he's God, I guess.

INQUISITOR.   If you were to see an apparition of the Father, the Son, and the Holy Ghost, who would you speak to first?

BAGATELLE.   I don't know, I guess the Son.

INQUISITOR.   The Son. Did you hear what he said, he said the Son. And you would not recognize the Father or the Holy Ghost.

BAGATELLE. Sure, I'd speak to them too if I could.

INQUISITOR. Bagatelle, what is the function of a good Christian?

BAGATELLE. To love and honor God as best he can.

INQUISITOR. And do you think that you loved and honored God by raping two innocent white girls?

BAGATELLE. I told you I didn't rape nobody. I ain't even screwed nobody. All I did was hobo on a train.

INQUISITOR. Have you ever been to Chartres, Bagatelle?

BAGATELLE. No, not me.

INQUISITOR. Have you ever made a pilgrimage anywhere? Or done anything other than wasting your substance among the Philistines?

BAGATELLE. I once went to a revivalist meeting with my mother.

INQUISITOR. Are you a man given to drink?

BAGATELLE. I drinks a bit.

INQUISITOR. Do you think you are without a soul when you get drunk?

BAGATELLE. No, I always know I got a soul.

INQUISITOR. That will be all. [*pause*] Wait. One more thing.

BAGATELLE. Yes.

INQUISITOR. How many angels can balance on the end of a pin?

BAGATELLE. Depends on the pin.

SPEAKER. Bagatelle carried a horseshoe with him into court. Everyone thought he carried it for luck, but actually he had planned to kill the Sheriff and make a getaway, if he was found guilty. There were, however, too many guards. The jury took twenty-six hours this time to find him guilty.

BAGATELLE. Goddamn! They done condemned me to death again. They sure don't like my ass in this state. Really.

SPEAKER. There was a certain high public official who was going to help in the release of the Scottsboro boys. Dr. Lazarillo, filled with the open sincerity for which he was so well-known, gained from this Public Official a promise of almost immediate release. At the last moment the Official found this course to be dangerous to his political career. Without informing Dr. Lazarillo he withdrew his support. The scene is in the office of the Official.

[LAZARILLO *makes a stormy entrance and addresses audience which is itself the* PUBLIC OFFICIAL.]

LAZARILLO. Hello sir, your secretary said you weren't in, but I didn't think we needed to stand on formality. We are after all old friends now, aren't we?

I've taken you at your word. I've promised those boys that they would be free by the end of the month. What do you suggest I tell them now? How could you betray them, how could you betray yourself like that? It was only a short while ago that we were speaking about philosophy, and law and religion, and now you've changed so utterly. It's as if you're two different people. It wasn't the pragmatist I spoke to two weeks ago, but a man with feeling, and knowledge of how those boys have suffered, for nothing essentially but the crime of birth. Don't look away from me like that, as though I were invisible or something.

Damn you! What can I say to reach your soul?
[*He stops, recognizing the impossibility of moving this now foreign person. He turns and walks swiftly out.*]

SPEAKER. The Public Official must be forgiven. He is the produce of an *ejaculatio praecox* birth.

SCENE THREE

[LAZARILLO *and* BAGATELLE]

LAZARILLO. Taking it like this will get you absolutely nowhere.

BAGATELLE. That's where you're getting me, absolutely nowhere.

LAZARILLO. Listen, we've had a good break . . .

BAGATELLE. I don't want to hear a damn thing, just leave me alone.

LAZARILLO. All right, Bagatelle, if that's the way you want it.

BAGATELLE. Did you bring me the cigarettes?

LAZARILLO. Oh yeah, here you are. [*gives him carton of cigarettes*] Look, Judge Nascitur is on our side, did you see how hard he tried to convince the jury in your behalf.

BAGATELLE. Yeah, he tried, everybody tried.

LAZARILLO.   It's just that the people here are afraid to be known as the one who condones the rape of a white woman.

BAGATELLE.   Why can't we move the trial up North?

LAZARILLO.   I'm not really certain that your chances would be much better there.

BAGATELLE.   Wonderful, ain't nowhere to go.

LAZARILLO.   Listen, I'm going to ask that you be examined by a psychiatrist.

BAGATELLE.   What's he going to do?

LAZARILLO.   You don't seem the same to me these days at all.

BAGATELLE.   I'm not the same.

SCENE FOUR

[*Six years later the* THREE SAD FELLOWS *are released on parole. The* THREE SAD FELLOWS *are freed from their chains; they form a row of three holding each other about the waist and start to dance about.*]

THREE SAD FELLOWS.   We're free, we're free,
oh what fun.
We're free, we're free
just like Lazarus.

I got shoes, you got shoes,
all God's children got shoes,
when we go to heaven
et cetera, et cetera et cetera.

[*The row of audience loses another two people,
who look on with disgust at the proceedings. Five
chairs are removed. There are now seven chairs
left, four of them occupied.*]

SPEAKER. The Three Sad Fellows went out into freedom, and
proceeded to lead lives of utter profligacy. Curiously
enough, nine years in an Alabama prison as a black man
is not the most conducive environment for learning
probity and good citizenship. Despite the meritorious
attempts of Dr. Lazarillo and others, the boys held few
jobs for very long. Nor were they moved to join the
NAACP, the Salvation Army, or any other noble institution, except for Sad Fellow Number One, who ex-
perienced a religious conversion, shortly before dying
from a kidney ailment.

They were known as wastrels and drunks. None to my
knowledge died in a state of bliss. Bagatelle said he
could hardly wait to become an alcoholic and a layabout.
Unfortunately he had to wait nineteen years before the
opportunity of escape presented itself.

After ten years Nicknack escaped but returned shortly
after getting his first piece of ass. The conversation went
as follows.

BAGATELLE. They got you, eh?

NICKNACK. No, I came on back by myself.

BAGATELLE. You did what?

NICKNACK.   Well, Dr. Lazarillo said it would be hard on you and Quid and Pro Quo, if I didn't give myself up.

QUID and PRO QUO.   Thanks, Nicknack.
Yeah, thanks.

BAGATELLE.   I always knew you was an asshole. You get out after ten years and you mean to tell me you gave yourself up for us.

NICKNACK.   Well, I sort of missed you, anyway.

BAGATELLE.   Is that right.

NICKNACK.   But I got some.

BAGATELLE.   You got some what?

NICKNACK.   Some pussy!

BAGATELLE.   Jesus! [*Pause. He stares out in wonder.*] I've done forgot what that is.

NICKNACK.   It was like you said.

BAGATELLE.   Is it?

NICKNACK.   We gone get out together, Bagatelle.

BAGATELLE.   No, we ain't. I ain't never gone get out unless I bust out. They got so many guards watching me I can't fart straight.

NICKNACK.   Dr. Lazarillo says there's still a chance.

BAGATELLE.   Don't mention his name to me. I finally figured him out. It bothered me cause I didn't know quite where to place him.

NICKNACK.   You understand white people real good, eh?

BAGATELLE. I don't understand them. I'm used to them, that's all. See if you start out realizing that they're out to kill you, you don't go too far wrong. Now they not gone kill you as long as they have some use for you. Only after.

NICKNACK. You think Dr. Lazarillo is out to kill us!

BAGATELLE. No, he's just crazy that's all. That's a complete other thing. He really is trying to help, he really does believe in justice. But he's going to be more of a problem to me than any of the others, cause all he does in the long run is get in the damn way.

SCENE FIVE

[*The leper-ship. The background of the stage suggests the outline of a ship. Atop hangs a sign:* NAVIS. BAGATELLE, NICKNACK, QUID *and* PRO QUO *are all holding lighted torches. The scene should suggest the prisoners as lepers on a ship of fools* (Stultifera Navis). *They are taunted by the other figures on stage, suggestive of various city and county officials.* DR. LAZARILLO *is also aboard.*]

BAGATELLE. [*holding torch in one hand and cigar in another*] Damn devil of a situation, ain't it?

NICKNACK. Water, folly and sea.
Water, folly and sea.

DR. LAZARILLO. We all remember what pretty Jesus said. How he'd some day wake us from the dead.

Coming then, with midnight choir,
taking sadness and desire.

QUID. Look, land, land!

PRO QUO. A port! A port!

BAGATELLE. Hoist the flag, boys. Nicknack, you burn some in-
cense. Tell the Three Sad Fellows to bring up the crosses.

QUID. Right.

PRO QUO. O.K.

BAGATELLE. [*trying to seem calm*] Ahoy there. Um . . . We're
a leper ship and I was just wondering if you'd sort of let
us stay in this harbor for a few days.

CROWD. Get the hell out of here.

BAGATELLE. Hey, listen, we won't be long, we disinfected everything.

CROWD. They have cracked stones. Don't let them in.

NICKNACK. Hell, my stones ain't cracked.

CROWD. They pissed against the wall.

BAGATELLE. What's a little piss between friends.

NICKNACK. Hey, Bagatelle, look, your mother, Bella Donna, is in
that crowd.

BAGATELLE. Where?

NICKNACK. [*pointing*] Over there.

BAGATELLE. Bella Donna, is that you?

BELLA DONNA. It's me. [*Only a voice is heard*] What did you do with the grocery money?

BAGATELLE. What grocery money?

BELLA DONNA. The grocery money you ran off with the day you took that train, and got your ass in so much trouble.

BAGATELLE. I don't remember no damn money.

BELLA DONNA. Don't curse at me.

BAGATELLE. Sorry.

BELLA DONNA. Are you eating all right?

BAGATELLE. Not too good, Ma. Been thrown out of twelve ports already.

BELLA DONNA. You should take better care of yourself.

NICKNACK. No way of taking care of yourself on these flood-ways, mam.

DR. LAZARILLO. They prove servants kind and good
    that sing at their work
    like birds in the wood.

QUID. Spent a score years away from our kinsmen.

PRO QUO. Prey to beast and foemen.

BAGATELLE. I sometimes try to walk as fast as the earth but somehow never succeed.

NICKNACK. Always twenty paces behind.

BELLA DONNA.   And what do you think about at night, my son?

BAGATELLE.   I think about the sun laying down for me.

NICKNACK.   Night is that darkness with eyes.

> [NICKNACK *turns about suddenly and sees* ELLEN
> TWITROMP *who is also aboard ship. They draw*
> *close to each other, stare for a long moment and*
> *then run off together.*]

BAGATELLE.   What? Where the hell are you two going?

BELLA DONNA.   What is your offense, my son?

BAGATELLE.   I've been improvident.

BELLA DONNA.   Oh.

BAGATELLE.   [*utterly bored*] I've disfigured the tabernacle and
grown sores on my flesh.

CROWD.   We're sorry for you all, but you can't enter here.

BAGATELLE.   Must I travel without tents and pavilions?

CROWD.   Yes.

BAGATELLE.   Addressing the help that will not come and the
tumult in the mountains.

CROWD.   Yes.

BAGATELLE.   Nothing out there but the screaming of the cuckoo
and the scent of the bittern.

BELLA DONNA.   Beware Egypt and the Indies.
> [BAGATELLE *looks out in amazement.*]

DR. LAZARILLO. When the hoar frost has gripped man's tent, then man will give thanks when night be spent.

SCENE SIX

SPEAKER. The 1940's was too crowded with various despairs for anyone to care about the Scottsboro boys. There was Hitler, then there was Hiroshima and Nuremberg and the Rosenbergs. People had no more sympathy left over, they had used it all up. Except for, of course, Bagatelle's mother who was never out of sympathy until she died.

MOTHER. [comes on stage.] Oh Lord, my son . . .

SPEAKER. High frantic atonal negroid wailing.

MOTHER. Oh Jesus, he never gone get out, never gone see me alive again.

[MOTHER is led away by two men. Two more of audience leave.]

SPEAKER. Thank you. And then in 1950 Bagatelle finally managed to escape to Michigan, where strangely enough he found sanctuary.

SCENE SEVEN

[*The Socialist Meeting Hall. A long table is prepared for a banquet, the guest of honor is* BAGATELLE *who is seated at center of the table. The scene is to conclude in Da Vinci's "The Last Supper." One* BEARDED FELLOW *is bending over by* BAGATELLE's *right shoulder as if to whisper something in his ear.*]

BANQUET HOST.   Well, ladies and gentlemen, I present to you the last remaining Scottsboro boy. He has successfully published a novel entitled *Scottsboro Boy*, heh, heh, heh, appropriately enough. Will you, please, say a few words, Bagatelle?

[BAGATELLE *stands and mouths words, but no sounds come out. Everyone is frozen in the posture of a painting.*]

SPEAKER.   [*walks over to* BAGATELLE] They can't seem to hear you.

BAGATELLE.   No.

SPEAKER.   How long has it been?

BAGATELLE.   Nineteen years.

SPEAKER.   Pretty long.

BAGATELLE.   Yeah!

SPEAKER. Do you know what's going to happen to you?

BAGATELLE. No.

SPEAKER. You will kill one of your own in a bar and go back to
jail.

BAGATELLE. Yeah?

SPEAKER. And you'll die of cancer in prison in two years.

BAGATELLE. Ain't that a bitch. [*puffs on cigar*]

SPEAKER. How would you describe your life?

BAGATELLE. My life?

SPEAKER. Yes, your life.

BAGATELLE. Fucked up, just all fucked up, from the get go.
Take out about one year of fun and you can cancel all
the rest.

[*Starts to walk off, notices the last two members
of the audience leave in outrage.*]

Yeah, that's what I said, fucked up.

[*This is said with utter calm.*]

Inside, outside, anyway you want it.

[*Turns to* SPEAKER]

In two years you say?

SPEAKER. Yes.

BAGATELLE.   And it's gone be cancer, eh?

[*The rest of the stage has fallen into darkness
except for the three figures,* AUTHOR, BAGATELLE
and SPEAKER.]

SPEAKER.   Yes, two years, cancer, and prison.

BAGATELLE.   I should have fought my way out the first day.

SPEAKER.   You wouldn't have helped the Fourteenth Amendment.

BAGATELLE.   Just all kinds of fucked up. Two years ain't that
a . . . [*walks off mumbling to himself, puffing cigar.*]

SPEAKER.   Ladies and gentlemen, *The Burghers of Calais.*

[*The spotlight falls on the seven vacant chairs.
The* AUTHOR *walks out slowly, hands again
pocketed. The* MUSICIANS *again enter, or record
is played: Dave Burrell's "Margie Pargie."*]

FUN
IN LETHE

(or THE FEAST OF MISRULE)

A British Tragicomedy

For Tyrone Gutherie

DRAMATIS PERSONAE

[*In order of appearance*]

BUM
HAMARTIA TCHENG, *West Indian poet*
MR. PENNFEATHER, *editor of publishing house*
TAN, *married mistress of Hamartia*
ETHEL BARZY, *Hamartia's aunt*
WALTER, *her son*
JOYCE, *her niece*
PETER, *her husband*
GEORDIE, *a Northumbrian singer*
USTAD, *a Pakistani*
SORDELLO, *West Indian writer*
TIRESIAS, *son of a Brighton butcher*
MOTHER, *Tiresias' mother*
BOATMAN
STRANGER
GIRL
ENGLISHMAN
BEGGARS
ATTENDANT
TOMAS TRUGOIDOS, *important personage in Irish theatrical life*
AENGUS
EUNUCH FOWL   *actors in Hamartia's play*
PETER THE WEST INDIAN
THE GOODLY SAMUEL, *Irish poet*
TONER, *owner of pub in Dublin*

The play involves the journey of a young Negro poet through Great Britain. The dramaturgic technique should be as simple as possible, thus contrasting the complexity of the character and the multiplicity of historical situations he recalls.

The drama makes use of Chinese classical drama (hence the Tcheng and Tan relationship) as well as Greek comedy—namely, the agon.

ACT ONE
SCENE ONE

[*London's Holland Park. On stage are seen park benches. Two of the benches are occupied by two sleeping figures, each beneath a blanket. A policeman comes sauntering by and kicks them awake as he passes. The first is an old white* BUM. *The second is a young Negro. The transport ballad of "Van Dieman's Land" is heard as the scene opens.*]

Welcome all you wild and wicked youths
wheresoever you may be.
I charge you pay attention
and hearken unto me.

It's the wicked, awful Transports,
as joy may understand,
and the hardships they do undergo
down in Van Dieman's land.

[*The* BUM *addresses the Negro,* HAMARTIA.]

BUM. Beautiful night, wasn't it?
Beautiful night.

HAM. Seemed pretty damn cold to me.

BUM. No, not too cold, mate. The moon was out last night, she
was.

HAM. The moon?

BUM. Aye, mate. And she was all big and yellow, and she put
a little shadow under herself, just as nice as you'd please.

HAM. Is that right! Well, I didn't notice.

BUM. Well, still, it makes a body glad to be about and kicking.

HAM. Kicking what, friend?

BUM. Why, kicking the gong, mate.
Kicking the gong.

HAM. [*shivering*] Christ, this is a cold country.

BUM. Why, it's April, mate, it's likely to be a bit drafty then.
Well, see you down at the Salvation Army tables. [*turns
and gives the upturned thumb symbol*]

HAM. Yeah, be seeing you.

[*exit* BUM]

[HAMARTIA *folds blanket, rests it on bench, then comes to front of stage, and addresses audience.*]

HAM.   "Whan that Aprill with his shoures soote
        The droghte of March hath perced to the roote."

[*pause*]

Morning from London's Holland Park. [*pause*]
This is my Arden.
Walk about and wait for the seven A.M., diurnal world of
England's working class to enter.
The sanguino-choleric faces of office men, taking
equi-distant, brisk, British steps toward labor.
The umbrella's held like a lance
the briefcases in left hands
rising in upward motion toward the breast.

[*pause*]

Office girls wearily pulling on synthetics about
themselves. And then . . . out, out to fields.
Come on, everyone, come on; forward labor,
stout hearts, you white-collar workers,
no slackening in the ranks.
Onward you Imports-Exports,
forward you home front men;
get that liberal to tighten his tie. [*pause*]
Better, much better. Capital!

[*stands back as if to let the imaginary parade
go by*]

Good show, good show, me hearties.
Briskly, briskly there, a little too much stomach,
that's better. [*Looks on proudly*]
All right, Wolf Tone, march them through the city center.

[turns and faces audience]

Hi there, everyone. Hamartia Tcheng here. My friends and intimates call me Ham. *[looks out into audience and waves at a girl]* Hi there, love. I'm a poet from the West Indies, that makes me a West Indian poet. I've lived in America and all parts of Great Britain, but on my passport it says that I'm a happy British child.

[sings]

How happy I am, I am,
how happy, lord, I am,
I am, I am, I am, I am,
oh lord,
how happy I am.
I've spent the last several months in London, and more especially in this park. And more especially still, on this park bench. *[pause]*
Still, I have not betrayed the goodly gifts. I've yet been practicing the craft of poetry. On those occasions, on those rare occasions, when I've been visited by the muse. Why, I was speaking to my muse just the other day. "Ham," she said—my muse always calls me Ham. "Ham, it don't say nothing in the union rules about my having to make visitations on a park bench."
So speaking, she left, and I haven't seen my muse since.
[walks about stage and his mood changes suddenly]

My morning activities consist of stealing milk from a doorstep—and thereby possibly depriving some poor British child of a morning drink of cow nourishment and also providing myself with food. Then by foot to Victoria station. There to see to my toilet and such needs, and then to uncheck what I must amusedly call my manuscripts. Three years of hunger and insanity to

produce thirty-six poems of brief length. And, with this
manuscript held bravely in trusting hands, I go forward
to a ten-thirty appointment with the chief editor of
Spilth Publishers.

[*darkness*]

SCENE TWO

[*The office of Spilth Publishers Ltd., England.
On the wall is hung the sign:* Defense d' Uriner.
On stage MR. PENNFEATHER, *an editor. He is in
his fifties, with gray, declining hair. He extends
his hand to* HAMARTIA *in welcome.*]

PENNFEATHER. Mr. Hamartia Tcheng, I presume.

HAM. Good day.

PENN. I'm very sorry it took so long to arrange an appointment.

HAM. Quite all right.

PENN. We're so swamped with manuscripts.

HAM. And here I am to swamp you a little more.

PENN. I've seen several of your poems in magazines. Very lyrical, very lyrical indeed. Of course, as you know one
doesn't make any money on poetry.

HAM. So I've noticed.

PENN. No, no, just can't be done. Is this the manuscript?

HAM. Yes. [*presents manuscript*]

PENN. Rather slim, isn't it?

HAM. Rather.

PENN. Well, of course, art isn't like vegetables. I mean you can't weigh it.

HAM. I guess you might say that insofar as a thing is written, it exists forever.

PENN. Yes, yes. My, that's rather good. We might just put that up. Insofar as a thing is recorded it exists forever. Quite. One thing that we might be able to do for you though is find you some kind of employment. We know that young writers often have difficulty surviving. How are you existing?

HAM. I'm not.

PENN. Oh. Well, come back next Wednesday and I'll see what I can find for you.

HAM. [*hesitantly*] Er, sir, I seem to be in rather dire circumstances, which is to say that my arse is to the wall. I wonder if it would be possible to secure five pounds just so I might get a little food.

PENN. Oh that bad, eh? Well, I was going to suggest something like that. Just wait here until I get our accountant, Barlow. Be back in a moment.

[*exit* PENNFEATHER]

[HAMARTIA *alone on stage looks out on audience.*]

HAM.   Praise God, I might survive yet. [*pause*]
       Maybe.

                                   [*darkness*]

SCENE THREE

[HAMARTIA *walks about stage.*]

HAM.   England is the inevitable conclusion of alliances. All of
       the disinherited bastard sons of the empire stumble about
       in a balmy night. The African, the West Indian, the
       Pakistani, the Chinese. [*takes several chairs up in hand
       and starts to arrange them strategically about stage*]
       This here is the river Thames. Flow gently, sweet Thames.
       Carrying with you a scent of blood and sinews. Here is a
       street where one witnessed executions. Over here is Bed-
       lam. Along here, Johnson, the good Doctor Johnson
       walked in search of reason.

       Here, along this part, is where the stout sons of England
       embarked for distant lands in search of honor and tem-
       perate climate.

       The intrepid sons of the Victorian age, who saw their
       duty and sport to change the lives of countless savages
       [*pause*] for the better. Carrying with them Christendom
       and cricket.

       I'll show you a nation that has traveled from feudalism
       to the vulvic taste of modernity without having given
       up a thing.

The Fowler's son has become the working man, content with his mutton of an evening, and his tele. The dealers in goods have begotten the dealers in goods. The leisure class has begotten the leisure class. How very tidy it all is.

They march on in careful sequestration through the ages, with occasional interruptions caused by the birth of some deviate, priest, artist, or military tactician, that step out of class.

Flow gently, sweet Thames, flow gently.

The murky waters of Hades flow out, and the blood-red waters of deeds return.

[*immediate darkness*]

SCENE FOUR

[*The hotel apartment of Hamartia. The room consists simply of tasteless paintings and flower-print wallpaper. On the floor are several books and a woman's fashionable dress. The woman is* TAN, *a wealthy wife and dilettante. She is about twenty-eight. Very attractive. She is stretched out beside* HAMARTIA *who seems asleep.*]

TAN.   [*after long pause*] Hamartia? [*pause*] Hamartia?

HAM.   Um?

TAN.   Are you sleeping?

HAM. Yes.

TAN. Hamartia, [*pause*] why are men so tired after?

HAM. I suspect it has something to do with the fact that you're insatiable, Tan.

TAN. You weren't so tired the first time we made love, you were quite active then.

HAM. Hmm.

TAN. Have you gotten used to me?

[HAMARTIA *turns, looks at her unbelievingly, then turns away again saying nothing.*]

TAN. All men want the same thing, to be surrendered to constantly, loved, pampered, told that they have the largest members in the world. [HAMARTIA *turns and looks at her again, then turns away as before.*] Avoid all responsibility, all pain, all . . .

Pam says ——

HAM. Who?

TAN. Pamela. You know, the girl I was walking with that day in the Haymarket?

HAM. The one who told me she'd like to eat me up?

TAN. Did she say that? Oh well, anyway she says that all women are just holes and that the sooner they realize it the better. [*Pause. She sees that she's getting no response.*]
Do you think that, Hamartia? Hamartia!

HAM. What, goddamn it!

TAN. I've made you angry. Do you think that women are just holes?

HAM. I've not done any thinking for some time now. Ever since I came to your country.

TAN. Our country, darling, you're a subject too.

HAM. Yeah, a subject for discussion, or at least comment.

TAN. [*laughing*] Don't blame me, the upper classes don't hate you, dear, it's the lower classes that are afraid you're going to take their jobs away.

HAM. Not me, I never work.

TAN. Of course, not that my parents are fond of you, but their dislike is generic rather than specific.

HAM. That's very comforting.

TAN. In any case, I like you very much.

HAM. That's also comforting.

TAN. Do you know what Charles said to me this morning——

[*lights cigarette*]

HAM. Don't tell me, it will only depress me.

TAN. Why, because he's my husband?

HAM. No, because he's absurd.

TAN. I never thought of that word for Charles. Absurd, very good. It sort of brings to mind a gaseous bag with feet. Absurd, yes, that's what he is.

Well, anyway, this morning he says, Tan, darling, you're looking rather sallow of late. Why don't you take a brief holiday in Majorca or someplace? What do you suppose he's up to?

HAM. He's your fantasy, honey, not mine.

TAN. "You're looking a little sallow." He's really priceless, that bastard.

HAM. I could easily see him paying several muscular men to break down my door and proceed methodically to break various members of my body.

TAN. Charles?

HAM. No, the several muscular men.

TAN. Oh, Charles couldn't care less about you. [*pause*] Do you think he would . . . care that much, I mean?

HAM. I ——

TAN. Hamartia! There's something crawling on my back. [*begins to squirm nervously*]

HAM. Hold still. [*slaps mosquito*] Mosquito.

TAN. Oh God, I'm going to break out all over.

HAM. From a mosquito?

TAN. I have very sensitive skin.

Oh God, I hate this place, how could you live here?

HAM.   Cheaply.

TAN.   And that man who owns this place——

HAM.   A nefarious Yugoslavian.

TAN.   I feel his eyes following me when I come near the place.

HAM.   There probably is no end of atrocities he'd like to commit with you.

TAN.   He's that type.

HAM.   Everyone is that type.

TAN.   You know, I could get a decent apartment for you easily enough.

HAM.   No thanks.

TAN.   But why not?

HAM.   You manipulate too well.

TAN.   All right then, stay in this grotey place and suffer.

HAM.   All right.

TAN.   But don't expect to see me here again.

HAM.   O.K.

TAN.   [*long pause*] Hamartia.

HAM.   Tan, if . . . if I should die—

TAN.   Yes.

HAM. See that my ashes are placed in the Abbey.

TAN. Last week you said you wanted your ashes dropped in the Thames.

HAM. No, I've decided in the Abbey.

TAN. All right.

HAM. Hmm.

TAN. I wonder what it would be like to be pregnant.

HAM. What?

TAN. My friend Noelle is having a baby. [pause] It must be funny to go about following your stomach.

HAM. Yes, lots of fun.

TAN. Well I wonder . . . I mean, it must be wonderful to have something going on inside you.

HAM. Starvation has the same effect.

TAN. Don't be so morbid.

HAM. Tell Charles you want a baby, something else that looks like him.

TAN. No, Charles doesn't go in for that sort of thing. At least not with me, if he has any overpowering urges he holidays in the Indies. I think he prefers your women.

HAM. Very British.

TAN. Very. [*pause*] I wonder if I'd waddle.
      Short women waddle.

HAM. You're not very short.

TAN. Well, I'm not very tall either. I mean, I might conceivably
      waddle.

HAM. Conceivably.

TAN. Waddle, waddle, waddle, waddle.

      [*They laugh.*]

HAM. You're mad.

TAN. [*Suddenly changes mood entirely. She stares at him for a
      very long time in dead seriousness.*] Hamartia.

      [*lights darken*]

      Again, again, again, a gain

      [*darkness*]

ACT TWO
SCENE ONE

[HAMARTIA *visits family at Nottinghill Gate.*]

HAM. [*Walks about stage; addresses audience.*] Nottinghill
Gate . . . used to be called Rottinghill, a coal dump.
Inhabited now by West Indians and exceedingly poor
whites. [*knocks on door*]
Hello in there.

VOICE INSIDE. What do you want? Who do you want to see?

HAM. Is a Miss Ethel Barzy within?

VOICE INSIDE. Ethel . . . it's for you.

[*Door opens.*]

HAM. Hello, I'm Hamartia Tcheng, Thomas' son.

AUNT ETHEL. [*an immense West Indian woman with a free laugh, massive arms upon which dangle several bracelets.*] Oh, me Lord, it's Hamartia. Come in, come in, son. Let me look at you. Walter, Joyce . . . Come; it's Thomas' boy, Hamartia. When did you arrive in London?

HAM. Er . . . a few days ago.

AUNT ETHEL. And you didn't come see us until now?

HAM. Well, I was, umm . . . trying to get myself situated.

[*Enter* WALTER *and* JOYCE. WALTER *is a well-built West Indian in his twenties and he looks like a laborer.* JOYCE *is an attractive light-skinned, straight-haired West Indian girl, looks about nineteen. The third person to emerge eventually is* PETER BARZY, *the husband of* ETHEL. *He is about forty-seven, well-built and in manner, like a skilled carpenter, sure and steady.*]

AUNT ETHEL. Walter, do you remember Hamartia? You were just boys when he left for America.

WALTER. Yes, I remember, I used to beat him up all the time. [*laughs*] How are you, man?

HAM. I'm still alive, I guess. [*looks very intently at* JOYCE]

AUNT ETHEL. This is Joyce Donoway, my niece. She just arrived from Barbados last November.

JOYCE. My pleasure.

HAM. You have extraordinary eyes, Joyce.

JOYCE. They're just eyes; I use them to see through.

HAM. Oh, how interesting.

AUNT ETHEL. Peter, come and see little Hamartia.

PETER. Well, well . . . he's certainly not little any more; he's a full-grown man. How are you doing, son? You look well. A lot like your father.

HAM. Thank you, sir.

AUNT ETHEL. Well, you must come and eat with us. Walter, get another chair from the bedroom.

WALTER. Yes, of course.

AUNT ETHEL. Let me take your coat.

HAM. Thank you.

[JOYCE *walks on and off stage as she sets table.*]

AUNT ETHEL. Where are you staying?

HAM. Near Holland Park.

AUNT ETHEL. Oh, not far.

PETER. Do you plan on staying in London?

HAM. I don't know. I haven't been able to come to any sense about the place as yet. I think I rather like Scotland.

WALTER. I've been to Scotland; it's too cold there, man. It's always raining.

HAM. Yes, but I think they have better places of learning.

WALTER. Oh, you're studying something?

PETER. Yes, his father always say, he is the one with the book.

HAM. Yes, well . . . I'm not studying as such. I mean, I write. Poetry in fact. I've been doing that for several years now.

PETER. And what do you do for a living?

HAM. I write poetry.

PETER. What? [*incredulously*] You mean you live by writing alone?

HAM. Yes.

JOYCE. [*entering*] What's so strange about being a poet? [*puts down plate*]

HAM. Thank you.

PETER. Yes, you are right. It's not that I believe there is anything wrong with this writer thing, but . . . um . . . it seems to me that a Black man would have great trouble. Do you know what I mean?

HAM. Yes, you're right.

PETER. I know.

WALTER. I don't believe in all of that. I mean books are all right, but in England what you need is a trade. If you can do things with your hands . . .

PETER.   And if you know the right people . . .

WALTER.   Yes, yes . . . the right people, too. That's always necessary. If you have these things in England, you can
survive.

HAM.   And, of course, it helps considerably to not be West Indian.

WALTER.   [*laughing*] Yes, very true. Don't be West Indian if you
can help it.

PETER.   [*seating himself before long table*] Ten years ago it wasn't
so bad.

AUNT ETHEL.   Joyce, bring in the yams and the peas when you
come in, girl. [*exit* JOYCE] Lord, I'm so tired these days
that I forget everything. Close the curtains there for me,
Walter. [WALTER *rises and goes to close curtains,* JOYCE
enters with two filled bowls.]

JOYCE.   Here you are then, Aunt Ethel.

AUNT ETHEL.   You shut off the stove?

JOYCE.   Yes.

AUNT ETHEL.   Hand me me sweater there. I'm still cold, can't get
used to the country, buddy.

HAM.   Yes, I know what you mean.

PETER.   When I first come here, my first winter, you know. Lord
. . . I wear me *puddin-draws* and three sweaters, with a
. . . what you call them shirts?

WALTER.   Flannel shirts.

PETER.   Yes, flannel shirts, a scarf and a heavy coat and cap, and me still was cold. Me ears burning me, man. I say, "But Jesus have mercy on me now."

WALTER.   Yes, your ears burn you, yes.

[*They all laugh.*]

HAM.   [*turning to* JOYCE *who is seated beside him*] You have beautiful legs, Joyce.

JOYCE.   Thank you. [*trying to seem unmoved*] I dance.

HAM.   Really? What kind?

JOYCE.   Classical, mainly.

AUNT ETHEL.   Yes, she's a very fine dancer. She wants to dance with the Royal Ballet some day.

HAM.   The Royal Ballet. [*almost childishly*] Yeah?

JOYCE.   You don't have to tell everyone, Auntie. Yes, I want to dance with them. I will someday.

WALTER.   You going to be the first black face in there, eh, Joyce Ann? [*laughing mockingly*]

JOYCE.   It has to happen, and when it does, I'll be ready. [*jumps up from the table and goes offstage to kitchen*]

AUNT ETHEL.   Walter, don't you make sport of her dancing any more. She works so hard. She comes from her job—she works at the tubes at Oxford Circus. And she comes home, eats and goes right out again to class. Four times a week.

PETER.   She'll make it, if she keeps it up.

WALTER. I was only joking; I know she's a good dancer.

PETER. That's a real West Indian woman there, she sure has a will.

[JOYCE *reenters with saltcellar in hand.*]

AUNT ETHEL. Well, let's say grace.

HAM. [*leaning toward* JOYCE] Do you ever go out on dates, love?

JOYCE. No.

HAM. Would you like to?

JOYCE. No.

PETER. Hamartia, why don't you lead us in prayer; you're the one that knows so many words.

[*They laugh.*]

HAM. [*startled at first; then relaxes*] All right. [*rises*]
God bless this house and all that's within
and God keep us all
away from our sin.
Keep out the night, the streets and the damp,
the poet who lives by grace and by thanks,
the layman, the scribe and the priest,
and may all at this table
their vantage increase.

AUNT ETHEL. Why . . . thank you, Hamartia.

PETER. Yes, very good, my boy.

AUNT ETHEL. Well, let's eat.

JOYCE. [*to* HAMARTIA] That was very good.

HAM. Thank you. I like you.

JOYCE. I'm glad . . . I think.

HAM. I'll come see you when you dance with the Royal Ballet.

JOYCE. All right.

HAM. I would like very much, I think . . .

JOYCE. What?

HAM. To stick my tongue in your ear.

JOYCE. [*quietly*] Don't say that.

HAM. Why?

JOYCE. Because that's not nice.

HAM. Oh, I'm sorry.

[*darkness*]

SCENE TWO

[*The Troubadour on Brompton Road.* HAMARTIA *is seated with two friends. A Pakistani,* USTAD MALIK, *and a large, bearded Northumbrian from*

Newcastle on Tyne named GEORDIE. *They are*
waiting for SORDELLO, *a heavy-set West Indian*
writer, connected with the B.B.C., who is very
truculent and rhetorical; his hair is almost totally
gone, and he vaguely resembles a Turkish fakir.]

HAM. So, we'll get the three quid from Sordello, when he gets
here.

GEORDIE. If he gets here.

HAM. Well, you know Negroes. They're always tardy for everything but birth and death.

GEORDIE. [*laughing*] Right.

USTAD. For birth and death, every man is early.

HAM. Ustad, you're quite the philosopher.

GEORDIE. I don't need philosophy; I've got the *Daily Worker*.
[*ironically*] I read it every morning, I do. I says to myself, Geordie, I say, why don't you read the *Daily Worker*
and find out what the bloody hell it is I'm supposed to
do today.

HAM. [*almost falling off his chair with laughter*] You do, eh?

GEORDIE. Indeed I do.

USTAD. [*solemnly*] The World is in a state of disrepair.

GEORDIE. Ha ha, he means it's ill-divided.

HAM. Why, yes . . . it is, Ustad, but just how much, you have
no idea. For example, Ustad, I'm going to tell you something. Now, I don't want you to panic. [USTAD *looks up*

surprised.] Do you know, Ustad, that you are in fact black?

GEORDIE. Oh God, here we go again. Why do you always get involved in racial arguments? You always put me on the defensive.

HAM. Now, Geordie, no need to get defensive. I realize that you can't help it, that you're white.

USTAD. [*calmly*] Hegel says, regarding the races of the world . . .

HAM. I don't give a pope's fart what Hegel says. Do you know that you are not white?

USTAD. Yes, I realize I'm not white, but I cannot properly say that . . .

HAM. To a white person, you are nonwhite. To be nonwhite is to be black.

GEORDIE. He's right, Ustad; that's the way that whites think.

HAM. And when will the Pakistanis learn that there is more to life than a dark suit.

USTAD. You want me to speak for my people. I cannot. For myself, I can say that I know there's more to life than a dark suit.

HAM. This whole country is going to explode soon—the inevitable conclusion of too much accumulated garbage. And everyone is going to say that it all doesn't make any sense.

GEORDIE. Yes, yes, the whole country is going to explode. Meanwhile, I'll keep working on my little song called "She was just a nice girl from Knightsbridge till she met her Soho love." It's bound to sell a million copies.

[*enter* SORDELLO]

SORDELLO. Midway in life's wood, I came upon a clearing. Clear the way, clear the way.

GEORDIE. Well, he's drunk as a lord.

SORDELLO. I am, sir, not drunk. I am sir, very drunk. Very, very very . . .

GEORDIE. Well, bugger-me, I've seen Sordello drunk.

HAM. I've been waiting for you for three hours.

SORDELLO. Um . . . terribly sorry, terribly. You see, I was somewhat trapped in a pub. Incarcerated as it were, behind seven double scotches. Very effective, very effective, that drink.

HAM. If you have that five quid that you owe me, perhaps I'll join you.

SORDELLO. I owe you three quid, sir, not five.

HAM. Just wanted to see how drunk you were.

GEORDIE. A West Indian never gets so drunk he forgets his money.

SORDELLO. Right. If for any reason anyone should ask after me, or the state of my mental health, say for me that I am *non compos mentis* and am thus having fun here in Lethe.

GEORDIE. Fun in Lethe.

HAM.   At last reports, Mr. Sordello was seen in a state of undress on Earl's Court Road.

SORDELLO.   Where he knelt naked atop rooftops of certain houses, in what he describes as an attempt to get nearer to God.

HAM.   You seem unusually gloomy tonight, Sordello. What happened?

GEORDIE.   I don't know; he doesn't seem unusually gloomy to me. He always looks kind of chapfallen.

SORDELLO.   Thank you, Geordie. Hamartia is, however, correct; my circumstance is unusually displeasing today.

HAM.   Do tell.

SORDELLO.   Well, how shall I say? I was relieved of my menial position with the B.B.C.

GEORDIE.   What he means is he was fired. What the hell did you do?

SORDELLO.   Well, my tooth and my tongue fell to mischance, and I told the truth to someone.

HAM.   Oh, tsk, tsk. Telling the truth again, Sordello. Good God, you'll never learn, will you?

USTAD.   What did you say?

SORDELLO.   Well, as you know, I've done two successful programs for the B.B.C. on West Indians and Africans. Everyone informed me of how fortunate I was to have had two programs for the B.B.C. under my—so to speak—belt. I was supposed to be in a state of primordial ecstasy.

GEORDIE. Or at least smile.

SORDELLO. I proposed, however, to do another one that really got to the heart of the issue. It was to be entitled *Of Calypso*. It was to concern itself with the history of the West Indies in general and the Calypso singer or Calypsonian, in particular. In discussing the project with my supervisor, I was foolhardy enough to admit to the insidious nature of the Calypso.

HAM. Ho, ho, ha, ha, ha.

SORDELLO. And said something to the effect of: the relationship of the West Indian to white is that of prisoner and jailer respectively.

GEORDIE. I don't think there's anything so radical about that statement.

SORDELLO. Well, I didn't either, but we are both unwise in dealing with issues of great pith and moment. For shortly thereafter, I was informed that due to a plethora of special programs, etc., etc., I would no longer be needed in the capacity of special writer.

USTAD. One must learn to avoid the thorns in life.

HAM. Lest they prick one, at one's rear.

GEORDIE. And a damn hard prick it is, too.

HAM. Well, you can still write for those West Indian newspapers.

SORDELLO. Oh, yes, do thrilling interviews with adjudicators, or their decision as to who is the best steel band.

HAM. The Pan Am Allstars, sir, the Pan Am Allstars.

GEORDIE. I don't know what you West Indians want. You've got steel bands, and we've even allowed you a cricket team.

HAM. Indeed you have.

GEORDIE. You people will want the bloody country next.

SORDELLO. I know it's terrible, you give them a taste of freedom, then there's no stopping them.

USTAD. Well, how does life in America compare?

HAM. America. Yes, well, America's a peculiar place.

GEORDIE. Darling place, really.

HAM. Yes, well, it's the sort of place where someone will come up to you and say, "I don't know if I like you; you look like you're thinking. I think I'll shoot you in the head." And then they do. That's pretty peculiar, don't you think?

SORDELLO. Very peculiar indeed.

HAM. But then, I come and see Southern England. And lo, what do I find!

SORDELLO. In all their splendorous ignorance.

HAM. Cloistered in their pubs, watching their rugby.

SORDELLO. Playing at their dreary game of darts.

HAM. And the worst country-Western music of America—the British.

GEORDIE. The Normans.

HAM. The progenitors of Americana.

SORDELLO. Hey, do that skit, Geordie.

GEORDIE. Which one?

SORDELLO. That British gentleman and the——

GEORDIE. Oh, yes. [*stands up and sticks out stomach like an affluent Britisher*] I say, lovely day, isn't it? [HAMARTIA *stands.* GEORDIE *speaks his words distinctly as though speaking to a Martian.*]

HAM. Which means it hasn't rained for an hour.

GEORDIE. Are you African, by chance?

HAM. Not of late, no.

GEORDIE. Seems odd, you know, that you're not African. I mean, have you seen Africa ever?

HAM. Only what I've seen in your movies.

GEORDIE. Most odd; I've lived for over thirty years in Africa. You can't imagine how beautiful it is.

HAM. I'm sure it was.

GEORDIE. What with the rosy-fingered dawn and the murmuring sea and what have you.

SORDELLO. And those callipygian little African girls, with their upward breast.

GEORDIE. It was [*pause*] healthier then, if you know what I mean. Well, I just wanted you to know that I have a very great feeling for your country.

HAM. Yes, I'm sure you felt her a lot.

SORDELLO. On every occasion.

GEORDIE. Ah, but you know this is a most strange country.

HAM. Passing strange.

GEORDIE. By God, I wonder where it's all going.

HAM. [*turning to deadly seriousness*] Nowhere, nowhere at all.

[*darkness*]

SCENE THREE

[HAMARTIA *at the apartment of* TIRESIAS]

HAM. [*walking to front of stage*] See the young poet
afoot in the streets
gives a little smile to all he meets.
Just like Jesus.

[*pause*]

Hope I live to thirty-six.
This is the home of Tiresias, the mordant. He's the son
of a Brighton butcher. Met him one day, as he was stealing light bulbs out of a hotel dining room.

TIRESIAS. [*A young fellow about twenty-five. He is seated in a
wheelchair, in dark glasses. On the walls are various charts*

of the human body. On the floor is a birdcage contain-
ing six blind mice. As the scene progresses, TIRESIAS *gets*
up from his wheelchair, quite relaxed] I was wondering
where you were; come on in, Hamartia.

HAM. I smell something good in the kitchen; food, perchance?

TIRESIAS. How is it that you're always hungry, man?

HAM. Because I never eat in this goddamn country. Only
Pakistani food, or when I'm at Nottinghill. The British
cook everything until it's safely dead.

TIRESIAS. [*calling to other room*] Mom, Hamartia is here.

VOICE FROM OFFSTAGE. Hello, Hamartia.

TIRESIAS. Says he's hungry.

VOICE. Well, there's some warm chops still on the table. Help
yourselves; I've got to get ready to leave.

TIRESIAS. [*wheeling about the room*] Go on in and get yourself
something.

HAM. Never mind then; I don't have the energy.

TIRESIAS. Damn, you're a lazy lot.

[HAMARTIA *throws something at him playfully.*]

HAM. So what have you been doing?

TIRESIAS. Waiting for life to abate.

HAM. As usual.

TIRESIAS. Yes, as usual. Bring the mice over here, please.

HAM.   [*grudgingly picks up birdcage full of mice and brings it to Tiresias*] Tiresias, why the hell do you have six blind mice in a birdcage?

TIRESIAS.   Oh, these are my sweethearts. These are. Just sort of sit here and watch the little darlings chasing their tails about.

HAM.   You're a curious fellow, Tiresias.

TIRESIAS.   You know, I've liked people much more since I've got these little fellows.

HAM.   You mean you like people now?

TIRESIAS.   No, but I dislike them less now.

[*The* MOTHER *of* TIRESIAS *enters. She is stout and about fifty. She wears a flowered dress and a black sweater.*]

MOTHER.   Hello, Hamartia. Well, I'm off to Ellen's, love. Oh, for God's sake! Tiresias, I told you to get those things out of the house. [*looking at mice*]

TIRESIAS.   Oh, they're no trouble, love.

MOTHER.   No trouble. Now listen here, I put up with that little what you call it——

TIRESIAS.   Baby's fetus.

MOTHER.   Yes, that "baby's fetus" that you had in that bottle for a year, but I simply will not tolerate these things in my house another day.

TIRESIAS.   All right, all right. [*Strokes birdcage*]

MOTHER. And get out of that wheelchair and stop making mockery of the paralysed.

[TIRESIAS *stands up.*]

TIRESIAS. Give me a kiss now, love.

MOTHER. Oh, all right. [*kisses* TIRESIAS] But see that you get them out of this house. [*exit* MOTHER]

TIRESIAS. You know my mom's a good peasant woman. They seem to abound in Great Britain.

HAM. I've noticed.

TIRESIAS. You know three years ago I was in Paris, studying psychology in the Sorbonne.

HAM. Really.

TIRESIAS. Until I flunk my final several times in a row. Can't make that cramming business. And then, bang, they take away my student card, my cheap lunches, my cheap movie seats. I was left to my own devices in Paris. Damn hard too.

HAM. I can imagine.

TIRESIAS. All I ever wanted out of life was to be left alone. To spend my existence in search of an effective vomitive against life.

HAM. It's your fault; you should have been born wealthy.

TIRESIAS. True. It's my fault. And now I'll have to give away my little darlings. Do you want them, Hamartia?

HAM. What, pray tell, am I to do with six blind mice in a birdcage?

TIRESIAS. Well, it can be your own little U.N., in a manner of speaking.

HAM. No thanks, I've got enough troubles.

TIRESIAS. [*quite seriously*] No, you don't. You have more than enough troubles. [*suddenly changes mood again, looking at birdcage*] This brown one here reminds me of a bird I once knew. Lived in Brighton, her father was a plant manager or something. Sort of consumptive, if you know what I mean. Thin shoulders and like that. Nice bird, though. Except she was always bleeding. Bled two weeks out of every month. Oh, me Mom will kill me if I keep them.

HAM. You could move.

TIRESIAS. What! And have to get a job! Not likely.

HAM. Just a suggestion.

TIRESIAS. I met this bird last week that wanted me to whip her.

HAM. Really?

TIRESIAS. I swear, I hate English girls; they're all daft. Whips and chains and what have you. She didn't look that sort, either. I mean, she was sort of a lumpish looking factory girl. Great legs, though. The type of girl you see coming out of the cinema alone on Saturday nights, embracing a soft drink or sucking on a polo.

HAM. Did you whip her?

TIRESIAS. No, I didn't have the energy. It tickled my id though.

HAM. I'm sure.

TIRESIAS. God, I've got to get out of this country. I felt alive in Paris. Starving, sure, but alive. Here, I'm just walking around inside my clothes.

HAM. Yeah, I'm going for a bit of trip myself. Thought I might take a look at Ireland.

TIRESIAS. Oh, God, Ireland. I've been there. Better make it a fast look.

HAM. Why?

TIRESIAS. Why, they're all crazy there. And poor as lepers. It's worse than London.

HAM. Well, I'll have to see for myself. People here are starting to call me by my first name. Pat me on the back and treat me just as if I was a human being or something. Which always means I'd better leave quickly.

TIRESIAS. You know what's wrong with you, Hamartia?

HAM. Yes, I know, but what do you think is wrong?

TIRESIAS. You, my friend, are cynical.

HAM. That's the wages of being born of the poor and unlettered.

TIRESIAS. Ha, ha. The poor and unlettered. Let's go down to the pub. I'll let you sport me a pint.

HAM. No thanks.

TIRESIAS. All right, I'll sport you a pint, same difference.

HAM. Okay.

TIRESIAS. Hey, come here; you've got to see my rope.

HAM. Your rope?

TIRESIAS. Yes, I call it Dr. Guillotine.

HAM. Why call a rope Dr. Guillotine?

TIRESIAS. It seemed amusing at the time.

HAM. Oh.

TIRESIAS. [*takes out rope, made in a noose*] I just sort of stick my head inside every morning and ponder.

HAM. Marvelous.

TIRESIAS. Can you imagine those executioners at Newgate?

HAM. As a matter of fact, no, I can't.

TIRESIAS. Well, they must have been a damn queer lot. Mothers telling their children hurry up and eat your porridge so we can go see the hangings.

HAM. Good British stock, I'm sure.

TIRESIAS. You know, I think I'll put these mice in the attic. Old Mom will never notice them there. Be right down.

[*exit* TIRESIAS]

HAM. God, I wonder what Ireland will be like. [*thinks of the multiplicity of possibilities and starts to laugh to himself*]

[*reenter* TIRESIAS]

TIRESIAS. Well, here you go then. [*presents* HAMARTIA *with a carved cane*]

HAM. A cane? Where did you get this?

TIRESIAS. Oh, stole it from a Druid Priest in Wales.

HAM. For me?

TIRESIAS. Well, you said you're going to dreary Ireland, didn't you? You'll need a cane there. And now you've got a sacred one.

HAM. Thanks. [*pause*] No, thank you is what I mean. [*offers* TIRESIAS *his hand*]

TIRESIAS. All right, let's be to the alehouse then. Are you one for drinking, me darling?

HAM. Aye, and verily.

[*darkness*]

ACT THREE
SCENE ONE

[*The Dublin night boat. The boat is crossing the Irish Sea. The stage floor represents the third-class compartment of the ship.* HAMARTIA *is stretched out on the floor beside the others. Some are writhing with nausea. To the right of* HAMARTIA, *a young couple in their early twenties are seated upon a small bench. They're locked in each other's arms attempting to sleep. As the scene progresses, a very nervous looking* ENGLISHMAN *appears in bathrobe and pajamas; he is obviously returning from some errand, probably for his wife; he steps apologetically over the suffering third-class occupants into his cabin.*]

HAM. Christ, it's cold. How can people live like this? Oh God, I've never felt so nauseous. [*pause*] Hey, excuse me there—

BOATMAN. Yes.

HAM. Do you work on this boat?

BOATMAN. I should say so, since I'm navigating it. My name's Charon. Been navigating for thirty years, sir.

HAM. Could you tell me how much longer it is?

BOATMAN. You mean the voyage? Why you've got another six hours at least. Takes eleven hours, you know. Well, see you on dry land.

[*exit* BOATMAN]

HAM. Well, God, perhaps I'll make it to the eleventh hour.

[*The young fellow sitting to the right of* HAMAR-TIA *with the girl looks up for a second, pauses, then asks* HAMARTIA *for a cigarette.*]

STRANGER. Hey, um, s'cuse me, mate, haven't got a fag, have you?

HAM. [*looks through his pockets, finally discovers his French cigarettes*] Here you are.

STRANGER. What's this? Foreign?

HAM. They're French.

STRANGER. Oh. [*taking one sort of frightenedly*] Thanks.

HAM. She having trouble sleeping?

STRANGER. Yes.

[GIRL *smiles innocently.*]

GIRL. It's so cold.

STRANGER. If we could be alone, I'd give her something to make her sleep well enough.

GIRL. [*blushing*] Tom!

HAM. Do you want this sleeping bag? You can use it for a blanket, or perhaps you'd be warmer lying on it.

STRANGER. Oh, not atall. Not atall. Don't you be traubling yourself.

HAM. No, it's really all right, this coat is very warm.

STRANGER. Not atall, not atall. [*looks at the girl who is shivering*] Well, if you're sure it will be no trouble.

[HAMARTIA *takes sleeping bag out of knapsack.*]

HAM. Here you are.

GIRL. Thank you.

[*Enter* ENGLISHMAN. *He passes by them after stepping on several people.*]

ENGLISHMAN. Ah. Terribly sorry. Terribly sorry. Sorry.

[HAMARTIA *looks at the other two, they smile.*]

STRANGER. This your first visit to Dublin?

HAM. Yes, yes it is.

[*Reenter* ENGLISHMAN. *He carries something in a red paper bag.*]

ENGLISHMAN. Umm . . . sorry, do excuse. [*turns around somewhat guiltily, then enters cabin*]

STRANGER. Ain't he a wonder . . .

[*One of the other figures on stage leaps up and goes in search of the toilet, to throw up.*]

HAM. Wow, this is a pretty rough sea.

STRANGER. Oh, she's calm tonight. The name's Tom McStephan. And this here is Ellen.

GIRL. Hello.

HAM. Hamartia.

STRANGER. Are you African?

HAM. No, West Indian.

STRANGER. Oh, yes. Studying at the college?

HAM. Yes, I probably will.

STRANGER. Good school—very good.

HAM. Did you go there?

STRANGER. No, but I know some people who did.

HAM. Oh.

[*darkness*]

SCENE TWO

[HAMARTIA *in Dublin*]

HAM.   Dublin, Ireland. Anna Plurabelle. Livia. The River Liffey.

[*A group of* BEGGARS, *children mostly, circle about* HAMARTIA. *He shakes his cane at them and pushes them away like an emperor.*]

BEGGAR.   Mister . . . mister . . . a threepence, mister.

HAM.   Away . . . away . . . you layabouts. You wastrels. Are there no prisons? Are there no workhouses?

BEGGARS.   Ah, fug off, you nigger.

HAM.   Out of the mouths of babes. Simply awful. Where was I? Oh yes; Dublin, Ireland. Anna Plurabelle. Livia. The River Liffey.

[*darkness*]

SCENE THREE

[*Trinity College vicinity.* HAMARTIA *is waiting for* TOMAS TRUGOIDOS. HAMARTIA's *play.*]

HAM.   Five months in Ireland. It's winter now and, therefore, people are nicer. [*pause*] Now I'm awaiting the arrival of one Mr. Tomas Trugoidos, an important personage in Irish theatrical life. He's coming to see a little verse play of mine entitled *Cormorants and Bitters*.

[*A small gray-haired* ATTENDANT *at Trinity College who holds a broom in his hand comes over to* HAMARTIA.]

ATTENDANT. 'Scuse me, sir. You write that thing? [*Beckons backward with his thumb.*]

HAM. Why, yes, I did.

ATTENDANT. Not bad.

HAM. Thank you.

[ATTENDANT *sweeps about a bit absentmindedly, comes back to* HAMARTIA.]

ATTENDANT. I used to know Brendan Behan. Used to deliver milk to him, before me leg went bad.

HAM. Really?

ATTENDANT. And Billy Yeats. [*pause*] And Jimmy Joyce, too. When he was living at that light tower with What's-his-face. Umm . . . Gogarty, the doctor.

HAM. Right.

ATTENDANT. Still he didn't do anybody any harm, you know. [*pauses and thinks deeply about his words*] He didn't do anybody any harm.

[*Enter* TOMAS TRUGOIDOS, *a heavyset, distinguished-looking gentleman clad in black corduroy jacket with belt and gray trousers. He checks his watch and apologizes.*]

TRUGOIDOS. Terribly sorry I'm late. You did especially say number three Trinity College.

HAM. It's quite all right. Won't you be seated? [*speaking to attendant*] Excuse me, can you tell Simon we're ready now that Mr. Trugoidos is here.

ATTENDANT. Which one's Simon?

HAM. Oh, he's the rather misused looking fellow with the cobbler's weak chest and the beard.

ATTENDANT. Oh yes, I know the one. [*goes offstage*]

TRUGOIDOS. What's this play, *Cormorants and Bitterns*, about exactly?

HAM. It's about [*pause*] birds and fish.

[*darkness*]

CORMORANTS AND BITTERNS

DRAMATIS PERSONAE

AENGUS, *Trinity College Student*
EUNUCH FOWL, *Retired Greek Professor*
PETER, *West Indian Watchmaker*

[*The stage consists of a huge pit with an over-hanging disposal chute for garbage; it is by this that* EUNUCH FOWL *makes his entrance. Betimes garbage falls from this chute. The characters all wear signs: the two white with the words "I am White," and the black West Indian with "I am Black."*]

ACT ONE
SCENE ONE

[AENGUS *is seen in foreground, the sleeping figure of* PETER *in back.* AENGUS *looks about overhead, stretches and speaks.*]

AENGUS. Dear Glory-father, I don't believe you exist, but just in case you do (one never knows in this halfway house of life), I ask you to remember me. Take my carrion body out of this stenchful place. I can't remember how long I've been in this bog. The nails of my fingers yellowed, my face etiolated, my body maggoty. [*garbage is dropped down the chute; his voice begins to screech*] Take me out of here. Oh Christ, I don't want to be a doughty lord in a carved house of jade, some ring-giver in a tidy hall. Just take me back to dirty Dublin, a place of much politics and little sex. Just a bit of chair beneath my arse in a silent pub, or sprawled out at Stephen's Green, a textbook beneath head.

Oh Jesus, how did I get here . . . I was coming from market . . . several porkpies and the bit of cod. . . .

No, that might have been the day before. Because I had failed the exam (should have known it was Traherne). "The Orient and Immoral Wind" or was it immortal wind? No . . . but I was walking out of Trinity among all those Norman women with lid-fallen eyes. The widow with the shawled child at her usual place at the corner . . . but how . . . Oh, God, I'm talking to myself. Eyes agley and back bent. I'll die here and some young medical student will find my skull and use it for a hat rest in his room. [*walks back and forth pondering*] Maybe this is all an experiment and they're watching me gleeful behind thick glasses. [*yells*] You unnatural bastards to make a game of man. [*composes himself*] Oh well, what is it anyway but a game with sad players. He knows [*points to sleeping* PETER] that Black heathen in the corner. Says I, "Don't you know we might die here?" "Not at all," says he. It's all one to him, says it gives him a chance to rest from women. Mad bugger. Oh God, my belly again. Best to forage about this slop, maybe lucky today. [*He crawls about on knees, picking up bits of rind and bones from about the floor. He crawls all around stage; after a pause, there is a shrill yell heard.* AENGUS *looks up startled.*] Mary and Joseph, what's that? [*Another cry, then body of man comes down chute head first. It is* EUNUCH FOWL. *His cane comes falling after him. He is clad in a gray tweed suit and tie.*]

AENGUS. [*rushing over to him*] Are you alive, man?

FOWL. Oh, mercy, what happened? I've been attacked. [*pushes Aengus' hand away, after noticing his filthy visage*] Get away from me.

AENGUS. All right. Be damned, you deserve to be here.

FOWL. Who are you, where am I? I demand to know. I'm a very important personage and this shan't go . . .

AENGUS. You're the dung of God is what you are. And so are we all that are here.

FOWL. I beg your pardon.

AENGUS. Oh, you have it, my Lord Pimple.

FOWL. I am Eunuch Fowl and demand to be addressed by title, regardless of where we are. Now I ask you again, tolerantly: where am I?

AENGUS. You're in the bog; it's the only name I can think of for this place. I don't know how you got here, because I don't know how I got here. The only thing I do know with any certainty is that you and himself over there are here, too.

FOWL. A most upsetting circumstance, this, however. I'm sure that it will soon straighten itself out.

AENGUS. That's the Normans, eternal optimists. Everything will straighten itself out by Monday morning, business day, eh? Oh God, do I have to suffer this, too? [*goes over to corner and seats himself on floor, his head bent in despair*]

FOWL. [*walking about, dusting off*] Frightful fall I had there; seem to be all right though. [*Lights begin to dim.*] Getting dark. A bit chilly, too.

AENGUS. That's what confuses you so, the days are so short you can't keep count. Tried a bit of system—marking off days—but it just depressed me, so I abandoned it.

FOWL. God, the dampness here.

AENGUS. Yes, the dampness.

SCENE TWO

[AENGUS *and* PETER *are still sleeping; it is morning.* FOWL *walks about.*]

FOWL.   I looked for a moon in the night, but there was no moon. [*Garbage falls from chute.*] Dark as Hades it was. Asleep I dreamt of Achilles, his bright armor stained with tears; in his hands the clutched staff, the wood hardened by the blood of wars. Chill from the mist of night. But it was not a new image. I have seen him before, in the backward hours of the night when death is aroused. The Irishman fears that we'll die here. Well, what are we tenants, heriot from the Gods, predatory and conspiratorial, with our face toward the sky and feet toward the gallows-tree.

Menen Aeide thea, Peleiadeo Achilleas Oulomenen, hi muri Achaiois Alge etheken, pollas d'ipthimous psuchas Aide . . . [AENGUS *gets up from sleep and is regarding* FOWL *speaking in Greek.*]

AENGUS.   What the hell are you saying?

FOWL.   Homer, good man that. What did you say your name was?

AENGUS.   I didn't. I'm Aengus.

FOWL.   [*conciliatory tone*] What do you do, Aengus?

AENGUS.   [*bitterly, yet ironically*] I live in the bog along with you and him and a lot of ants.

FOWL.   [*well composed*] Fine creatures, ants; they most resemble Plato's *Republic*. I say, what do you do for food here?

AENGUS.   Ha ha, there it is all around your feet. Sometimes you're lucky and you can corner a rat, but mostly it's the effluvia coated with the sperm of dogs that you eat.

FOWL.   Come on, man, you don't mean . . .

AENGUS.   [*crawling about, picking up scraps*] No, I'm joking. It's all a big joke; you're not really here, and that's not your stomach rumbling.

FOWL.   Man, the cacophagic animal with voice. [*looks on, as* AENGUS *crawls about*]

[PETER *gets up for the first time and stretches, looks about him and laughs as he sees* AENGUS *and* FOWL *very demurely bending after unsuccessfully trying to lift an apple peel with his cane.*]

PETER.   Well, well, Aengus-Pengus, I see we got company. [FOWL *looks up aghast at the sight of* PETER.] Night mister.

FOWL.   My God, he's black.

AENGUS.   [*turning around on his knees*] Don't be a bloody ass, man. I think there's part of an orange by your foot.

FOWL.   No, no, he's black, and he looks healthy.

PETER.   Yes, I'm black, mister. You've got eyes. Since I've been here, I've been in a nice disposition, so don't get me angry, mister. Be nice now and don't say anything rude or Peter will have to lay hold on you.

[AENGUS *starts to wretch violently and vomit.* PETER *goes to his assistance.*]

FOWL. Look, as long as you're here you'll take orders for me. . . . I mean us. We must have some semblance of commonwealth here. Insofar as we must maintain a contiguity and society. Now you will take your meal and necessities after us. I think it best also that you sleep by the North wall, Aengus by the right and I in the center. We shall have to do something about sanitation also. Hmmm . . . yes, all human waste shall go in that corner. . . . Yes . . . and wait, Aengus, don't vomit there.

PETER. Don't pay him no mind, Aengus. Ha ha, the fool is crazy. [*helps* AENGUS *to his feet*]

AENGUS. Look, Fowl, we've been getting along very well up till now (except for the wretching), before you got here. Now if you don't mind, please, keep your comments to yourself. You're not in your country or your university now.

FOWL. [*going over to* AENGUS] You'll see I'm not wrong.

SCENE THREE

[AENGUS *and* FOWL *are seated at one end of the stage and* PETER *at another.* FOWL *gets up and walks over to* PETER, *tapping his cane.*]

FOWL. Tell me, Peter, what exactly do you want to do?

PETER. [*not looking up*] Stay alive, mister.

FOWL. I mean, if and when you get out of the bog.

PETER. I would like to be a watchmaker in a distant town, filled with big women that look like they're dancing when they're walking. Have all my clocks ring out wild at twelve o'clock, then no one would know if I'm crazy. Ha ha.

FOWL. Strange profession, watchmaker.

PETER. I played with clocks since I was a child. One day my father caught me opening his old watch; he told me, pull down your pants, boy, and let me see how old you are.

FOWL. Really. [*walks back to* AENGUS]

AENGUS. You look like you've got an evil mind.

FOWL. Listen, Aengus, you know what we are.

AENGUS. I can remember . . . It doesn't seem that long ago, sitting with a girl on the green, you know? An awkward girl, thickish, always with a scent of lime. She worked in a laundry. I think her name was Suzanne . . . or was it Jane?

PETER. I remember a girl named Jane. She smelled like fish though. Always smelled like fish when we made love.

FOWL. All of this is very interesting, gentlemen, but if we might just get to reality for a second. Now then, we must send a message, some sort of indication of our plight. There must be some way.

AENGUS. What shall we say? Perhaps we are displeased . . .

no, no, rather we are in dispirit here. Would you mind awfully ending this absurd game?

PETER.   Tell them there's no rum here, or women.

AENGUS.   And no clocks.

PETER.   Right, right, there are no clocks to fix.

AENGUS.   Or perhaps we three were a synod of clergy. One of us a Pope. You would like terribly to be a Pope, wouldn't you, Eunuch? Yes, we shall send a great encyclical, a churchful to them—the laity out there with their clean hands and boring faces. All their teeth gleaming with pleasure at our suffering. Yes, that would be good.

AENGUS.   We must speak seriously, from a council.

PETER.   Can I be on your council, mister? Hey, mister, why are you so dull? You're such a little man with your little suit and stick. Your funny little dull face. Can I be on your little council, mister?

AENGUS.   What shall we say? We must say something. Something important. Something like, we are lonely here, we three. Lonely with ourselves. The yourself, the myself, the ourselves. Lonely among the rinds and pits.

FOWL.   Over there lies the only threat to our security. [*points at* PETER]

AENGUS.   You're the only threat I see.

FOWL.   We have to think about our food supply. And how do you know he doesn't resent our being white, our being masters. Besides, if there were only two of us the available food would be greater.

AENGUS. For God's sake . . .

FOWL. I say deal with him before he deals with us, like the baying wolf.

AENGUS. Firstly if he does kill us, what of it? What are we living for, to vomit over our own bodies, to sleep in our own dung? Secondly, if someone has to be eliminated, I don't see why it has to be him instead of you. He at least has some song about him. You, running round with all your fantasies of gods and ants. Look around you, man; this is no empire; it's a filthy sewer. You see that thing crawling there, it's a worm, and soon it will be crawling over you, but you won't see it because the night will shadow you. How many worms have already gone into your body; how many dead men?

FOWL. So that's the way it is.

AENGUS. That's the way of it. So let's hear no more of your gibberish about Aristocracy.

[*Stage lights dim.* AENGUS *begins to sing sleepily.*]

AENGUS. There were three ravens sat on a tree
Down a down, a derry down.
There were three ravens sat on a tree
Hey ho
There were three ravens sat on a tree
They were as black as they could be.
A down, a down, a derry down.
Hey ho.

[*repeat first stanza*]

The midmost raven said to me
There lies a dead man in a tree.
A down, a down, a derry down.
Hey ho.

[*He sleeps.* PETER *is also asleep.*]

FOWL.   Yes, that's the way of it. Dark Zeus, guard my step. Lady Helen, tender and Ionic.

[*He steps quietly over to* PETER *and strikes him several times with his cane.*]

We must have order, deal with him, lest he deals with us.

[FOWL *now walks over to* AENGUS *and clubs him, too, with the cane.*]

It was lamentable but necessary. I know it shan't be long before I'm missed. They'll send search parties after me. . . . Perhaps the nocturnal guards. No other way to deal with the situation. When one is among fools, one must take command. . . . A watchmaker, indeed. Soon I'll be home with the morning paper . . . the mailman with sweaty brow. Leave a shilling for the boy. . . . God, the dampness here. . . . Move their bodies closer for warmth. [*drags bodies together about him*] Must sleep . . . maintain strength . . . the stench . . . the stench.

[*sings*]

There were three ravens on a tree
A down, a down, a derry down.
There were three ravens on a tree
Hey ho.
There were three ravens sat on a tree
All as black as they might be.
A down a down a derry down.
Hey ho.

[*curtain*]

SCENE FOUR

[HAMARTIA *and the* GOODLY SAMUEL. SAMUEL *is
an elderly Irish bard; he sits bent like a dying
flower. As* HAMARTIA *prattles,* SAMUEL *pays little
attention. They are at* TONER's *Pub, on Merrion
Road.*]

HAM.   Got a letter from Tiresias today. Said that my lady friend,
Tan, got married again to a Mr. Tchou, some owner of a
munitions factory or something.

SAMUEL.   Ummm.

HAM.   Got the four hundred dollars from America, too.

SAMUEL.   [*shakes head in agreement*] Ummm. . . .

HAM.   Could I get you another?

SAMUEL.   Don't trouble yourself.

HAM.   My pleasure; I'll be leaving soon.

SAMUEL.   You know . . . there is, I'm thinking, a sort of tiredness to the world. [*looks up and calls out to barkeep*]
Would you say so, Mr. Toner?

TONER.   [*a balding, serious Irish bar owner*] Wouldn't I say
what, Samuel?

SAMUEL.   Would you not say that there is to the world a certain
tiredness. A sort of overweary state of things, somewhat
like two dying athletes who have discovered themselves
to be in a circular tract with no point of finish?

TONER.   I've never found it like that, no.

SAMUEL.   No, perhaps it's just me own malady. I can't help but wonder sometimes, though, if perhaps it's some error I made. At my birth, I mean. Perhaps some vow unfulfilled or hecatomb unworshipped. Or perhaps a genuflection unmade in a cathedral. Some little things I must have forgotten in all my doing.

TONER.   And why do you say that?

SAMUEL.   Because I come upon my own and my own knows me not. And those whom I don't know also find me foreign.

TONER.   How do you mean?

SAMUEL.   Well, take for example these things that I do . . .

HAM.   You mean your poems?

SAMUEL.   I call them things, that suffices. Now when my countrymen come upon them they say, me God, the bloody man's daft, he must be mad as a hatter to do that.

TONER.   The world's a curious place, there's no denying that.

SAMUEL.   Ireland's the curious place. I've been to the large cities, about the world I mean, and I've seen the rain falling downward and the women standing at their windows alarmed.

HAM.   I have to get out of Great Britain altogether; my mind's turning to dust.

TONER.   Why don't you feel safe here, lad?

HAM.   It's not safeness that I feel here, no.

SAMUEL. My country's a betrayer.

TONER. No betrayer, no, you can't call her a betrayer. It's them that goes away from her is the betrayer.

SAMUEL. Stay and she won't let you live.

HAM. She'll let you live, but she damn sure won't help you.

SAMUEL. Still, you can't ever forget her. She's like your navel or your arse or something.

HAM. Well, fuck all and up the I.R.A. I say.

TONER. Who asked you?

HAM. Well, no one, but if they were to, that's what I'd say.

SAMUEL. I had a dream the other day.

HAM. Which day?

SAMUEL. Oh, it doesn't matter, some day in the past surely.

HAM. Yes.

SAMUEL. That I had come upon a sort of village, a strange place with broken roads. And I asked those I met the way to the death house but none could tell me. There were these children though, and they were all very beautiful, with the kind of circular faces that country children have. Save for one boy, who was misshapen and walked with a staff.

HAM. With a staff?

SAMUEL. Yes, but he couldn't tell me the way either.

TONER. I haven't dreamt for a great while now.

SAMUEL. Odd that I can still dream, you know. I mean, one falls asleep after one has done as much damage to the self in one day as one can. I mean after you've killed off as much living things as possible, flies and insects and such.

TONER. Yes, yes.

SAMUEL. After you've displaced as much grass as possible with your footsteps. You sleep, and it's a wonder that you still have energy enough to dream.

TONER. It's a wonder indeed.

SAMUEL. Then you wake and find your brutish and sweating self all ready to start the assault anew, all over again.

TONER. God be praised.

SAMUEL. Of course, what really bothers me, you know, is man's likeness to the rat. Does that bother you, Mr. Toner?

TONER. Not at all, not at all.

SAMUEL. I mean, we both copulate out of season, can adapt to any climate, fight alone or in groups; and this point especially—will easily enough kill another of the species.

TONER. A rat has a tale surely.

SAMUEL. Still it's all very disturbing. The first rat in Europe returned with the crusades.

HAM. Couldn't you just see him, plump and holy.

SAMUEL. The rat in number is the only thing which equals man. And is, I'm given to understand, wholly parasitic.

TONER. I suppose they'll win in the end.

HAM.   Yes, but then they'll have to wipe each other out.

TONER.   That's true, you know.

HAM.   Well, God bless you, everyman.

SAMUEL.   [*lifting glass to head*] And Christ your portion be.

[*darkness*]

SCENE FIVE

[*The stage suggests a train moving at night. Flickering shadows.*]

HAM.   I think it's four days now that I've been on this railway. Each time we stop the voices change. Women come. Girls come, on and off. Wearing green or yellow shoes. The shadows of dreary industrial towns, or futile agricultural towns. The ground moves backward then.

[*pause*]

You can tell the night from the day because it's more damp then and the voices are more silent.

It will be spring again probably.

I have spent the night solitary [*pause*] and without incident.

[*curtain*]

THE
MUMMER'S
PLAY

Dramatis Personae

[*In order of appearance*]

DEMOSTHENES BELLYSONG JONES, *retired Negro sculptor*

NEMESIS JONES, *wife of Bellysong*

BO-SIMON, *friend of Bellysong*

PARIAH ANON, *poet friend of Bellysong*

MISS NANCY RILEY, *mistress of Bellysong*

ANNE, *girl friend of Pariah*

FELLOW IN CROWD

CHORUS

ST. PETER

FIRST ANGEL

SECOND ANGEL

SOL FINKLESTEIN, *Anne's father*

MRS. FINKLESTEIN, *Anne's mother*

NEGRO MAN

SCENE ONE

[BELLYSONG *introduces himself. Thelonious Monk's "Straight No Chaser" is heard throughout.*]

BELLYSONG. Likewise that morning, Mr. Demosthenes Bellysong Jones (Bellysong among his chorus) walked through the dark and half-dark of the five A.M. world of Harlem's dawn streets toward his dwelling at the basement apartment of 1876 West 116th Street. He licked the corners of his lips for the last tavern taste of beer, looked with contentment at the poetry of the deserted streets and the few lit apartment windows, and started his descent to the basement.

At the bottom of the stairs, he took nimble steps, walking upon the long plank thrown over the large puddle of water (caused by the sewer stoppage), that he or his friend Pariah had once called "The Thames." [*Nods in agreement*]

Having successfully reached his door, he fumbled within the pockets of his worn corduroy pants and, after finding every variant of effluvia, discovered the small metal key.

Entering. Facing him: flowered wallpaper upon which is hung a plaque with the words: HOME IS WHERE THE HEART IS; a worn green carpet between kitchen and living room; artificial flowers on the table; a worn yellow chair with matching sofa (as yet unpaid for, although already broken); a Singer piano with an absence of four keys.

He made straightaway for the kitchen, started water boiling on the one workable jet of the stove, and withdrew the evening paper from his pocket.

He was not a large man, five foot six or seven, but he had a commanding face, especially because of his short thick mustache—"the symbol of the Southern gentleman," he would say. Indeed, all about him radiated civility and gentility save, of course, for his corduroy garb with baggy and overlong trousers. His speech was ornate and plenty—commonly it was said of him that he made a volume out of any description needing five words. He could certainly have been a success in this world instead of just a massive phenomenon, were he not, as he said, "so unmistakably Negro and moreover poor."

[BELLYSONG *sits in the squeaking brown chair, scratching his large head and turning the pages of his newspaper hurriedly to the obituary column. A high, piercing voice calls from the dark of the inner room.*]

SCENE ONE   125

NEMESIS.   Is that you, Bellysong?

BELLYSONG.   No, it's drunken Jesus come to take you away from the sins of the world.

NEMESIS.   Always got some wise-ass answer but you can't get your behind home at night so you can wake up and go look for a job like everybody else, can you, professor?

BELLYSONG.   Nemi, please, go to sleep. I'm not up to repartee at this damn hour of the morning.

[*A few inarticulate grumbles are heard and then silence.* DEMOSTHENES *reads aloud.*]

BELLYSONG.   "Cathleen Thompson, beloved wife of Henry Thompson, mother of Agnes and Gail Thompson. Services Sunday the nineteenth at Benthas' Funeral Home." Hmm, so the old girl finally departed. Guess Henry will be able to get around to the club now. Hideous case of constipation she had. Ashes to ashes, etc. Christ, the damn stove's gone off again. [*He scrambles for a match, lights stove. Loud bang. He turns off stove, waits, lights it again, returns to chair.*] Hmm, maybe, Mrs. Nemesis Jones, faithful wife of Bellysong Jones, mother to Alfred Jones. Simple services to be held at the Harlem River, cremation followed by scattering of ashes to the four winds to ensure equal distribution of essence to the various spheres of the globe. [BELLYSONG *laughs hysterically, causing the chair to squeak. He grabs hold of the table to keep himself from falling backward.*]

NEMESIS.   Bellysong, will you get yourself to bed. I'm the one who gotta get up and work in an hour, while my no-good, lazy-ass husband stays home making toy elephants like some goddamn kid.

126   **THE MUMMER'S PLAY**

BELLYSONG.　Oh Lord, how long?

[*Rises, turns off still unboiling water, pulls the light switch and retires to the living room. Takes off jacket, lays it across back of chair, and lies down on couch still wearing trousers and shirt. Pulls blanket over him. Outside can be heard the sounds of garbage cans being thrown, horns of cars, and sounds of feet entering the diurnal world.* BELLYSONG *crouches in fetal position and begins to snore.*]

[*darkness*]

SCENE TWO

[*Two hours later*]

NEMESIS.　Bellysong, Bellysong.

BELLYSONG.　Christ Jesus, what, damn it?

NEMESIS.　Look out for Con Edison today. I had a dream about the inspector coming. And pick up some food, for God's sake, the icebox is empty.

BELLYSONG.　And what the hell should I pay them with, the synoptic gospels?

NEMESIS.　What should you pay them with! Well, what did you do with that unemployment check you got last week?

BELLYSONG.　I've got expenses, woman.

NEMESIS. Yes, you got expenses at that goddamn bar at 125th Street is where you got expenses. Thank God Alfred joined the army, otherwise he'd still be depending on me. You never gave him a damn thing.

BELLYSONG. Yeah, from what he says he's having a ball in that army too, if he doesn't get himself killed in Saigon.

NEMESIS. Oh Jesus, I'm late. Remember what I said about Edison. Hey, Bellysong, when is Pariah coming back?

BELLYSONG. If he had any damn sense, he'd never come back to America, but he's supposed to be back sometime this week.

[*Slam, sound of door being locked. Inarticulate cursing as feet try to balance themselves on plank leading to upstairs.* BELLYSONG *sleeps.*]

SCENE THREE

[*One o'clock the same day. Sound of rapping heard at door,* BELLYSONG *turns over and ignores it. Knocking gets louder,* BELLYSONG *panics, remembering Edison.*]

VOICE. Hey, Bellysong, it's Bo-Simon.

BELLYSONG. Oh, it's you, Bo. Hold on, I'm coming.

[BELLYSONG *opens, greets* BO *with full set of smiling teeth.* BO-SIMON, *a man in his early forties, largish, weighs about two hundred*

*pounds, looks like a small-town, Negro Sidney
Greenstreet, light-skinned, straight hair, with the
rotting green teeth of a debauchee. Always
carries a cane for knocking at doors or affecting
the war veteran's* Miles Gloriosus.]

BO-SIMON. Good God, man, doesn't the landlord know that
sewer's out there stopped up? It stinks and somebody's
going to fall and bust their ass on that thing.

BELLYSONG. Well, I don't mind. I think it gives an atmosphere
of the Arthurian Age, you know, with moats and castles,
etc.

BO. You out your damn mind. This ain't no castle, this whole
place is one big outhouse.

BELLYSONG. No, friend, America is one large unflushed toilet, of
which this is only one small section in the underpipes.
[BELLYSONG *laughs, leaning against chair for support.*]
So how's your love life these days, Bo?

BO. Well, you know how these damn high yellow Southern girls
are. They either want money or a wedding ring before
they get up off some trim, and since I've been, as you
would say, in a rather impecunious situation . . .

BELLYSONG. Indeed.

BO. It's been kind of slow. Hey, by the way, my wife's hunting
me down again, I understand.

BELLYSONG. Your wife, now there's a gentle woman. She has sense
and understanding and knows how to give a man
freedom. I don't know what ever possessed you to quit
that girl.

BO. Well, I'll tell you, Bellysong, that pot of boiling hot water she almost scalded me with had something to do with it.

BELLYSONG. What the hell do you expect with you whoring after all those women, leaving that poor girl at home with the two kids?

BO. Look, Bellysong, you don't know a goddamn thing about my wife and me. Now I know I ain't no angel but I'm a humanist. I believe in treating everyone right . . .

BELLYSONG. Oh yea, Bo-Simon, the humanist always ready to give everyone an equal jig up the cheeks, ha ha.

BO. Well look, you ain't in no position to talk about anybody. I heard how you been chasing Miss Nancy Riley, that old heifer, and that Deacon Perkins' wife . . .

BELLYSONG. Jesus Christ, a man can't even fart without it being published.

BO. So you can't go telling anybody how to act ethically concerning women.

BELLYSONG. All right, all right, look, we're two anachronisms, two Renaissance men locked in an outhouse. We're college men, we shouldn't have to be crucified by dumb empty . . .

[*Bang, bang, loud knocking at door.* BELLYSONG *quietly shuts kitchen light. The two men sit silent in the dark kitchen. Knock is repeated followed by a knock more distant.*]

VOICE 1. Yes?

VOICE 2. I'm looking for a Mr. Demosthenes Jones. Con Edison calling.

130 THE MUMMER'S PLAY

VOICE 1.   Well, he lives next door.

VOICE 2.   Yes, well, he doesn't seem to answer. Do you know if he still lives here?

VOICE 1.   I think. They say he went on a vacation to Florida for the winter. You know, "come on down." Ha ha.

VOICE 2.   Very *amusing*. Will you tell him for me that next time I'll bring the authorities and we'll take out that meter of his whether he's at home or not.

VOICE 1.   Kiss my black ass.

[*Slam of door. Young man standing amazed looking at shut door, fixes hat on head and attempts to cross plank to stairs. Puts weight too much on one side. Cry of "Oh my God!" Splash.* BELLYSONG *inside on floor paralyzed with laughter, holding on to* BO's *leg for support, trying to suppress squeals. Sound of feet ascending stairs.*]

BELLYSONG.   The bastard fell, did you hear him? "Oh my God," ba bam. Ha ha.

[BO *leans on chair, holds head.*]

BO.   Oh Christ, I've laughed so much I got a headache. Hey, you have any coffee here, man?

BELLYSONG.   Oh God, beautiful, ga blam. Ha ha. Yea, there's some coffee, I think, unless the old hag threw it out to spite me.

BO.   Here it is.

BELLYSONG.   Good. Now if you can live long enough for the one jet to finally heat up that water we'll have some.

BO.   Hey, Bellysong, why don't you get one of those Economic Opportunity jobs? You know the government's starting to feel guilty about treating Negroes like pigs for so long that now they got all sorts of openings in these teaching projects. You could bullshit your way into one of those. That is your forte, isn't it?

BELLYSONG.   What, and get involved in one of those sedentary jobs with those Bostonian Negroes that act like they've got brooms stuck up their asses because they're so frightened they might get caught being natural Negroes?

BO.   Yeah, I know what you mean. My flesh crawls when I get around those hairless bastards. [*pause*] Of course, I wouldn't mind joining them though. Jesus Christ, it's freezing in here! Why the hell don't you take the landlord to court, Bellysong?

BELLYSONG.   Oh yes, indeed, that's my beloved wife's answer also. May I remind both her and you that we're three months behind in the rent; never mind the fact that he is aware of a few of our indiscretions, to wit: the jumper in the gas meter he found, and our telephone being connected on the Thomas' wire upstairs. Under the circumstances I think it best to wait for a more propitious moment, don't you? I have, however, been reading the obituary column daily, waiting to hear that that bad heart of his finally gave out and that he's shuffled off his mortal coil.

[*The sound of feet coming down the stairs followed by a loud clear oratorical voice*]

PARIAH.   Oh for joy, methinks I see the river Thames. What ho there. Make way for the Nazarene.

[BELLYSONG *rushes to door, embraces the young figure holding duffel bag high.*]

BELLYSONG. Pariah, I was wondering when the hell you'd show.

[PARIAH ANON, *a youth in his early twenties; pompous look omnipresent on face, save for brief smile and thick shattering laughter; holds pipe in right hand always swept forward for emphasis in a falciform motion.*]

PARIAH. Hello and well met, Bo. How are you?

BO. I ain't good as you, that's for sure. I can't go to Europe.

PARIAH. One can never go to Europe, sir. One must just go.

BO. One might just find one's ass in jail in Europe too, baby.

PARIAH. I think that somewhat easy to do in the United States also, don't you, Bellysong?

BELLYSONG. Bite your tongue, boy. This is my fatherland you speak of. Ha ha.

PARIAH. I see that the moat is still present outside. As a matter of fact, everything is still the same.

BELLYSONG. Like I said, one unflushed stagnant toilet.

SCENE FOUR

[BELLYSONG *and* PARIAH *are seated together alone in the kitchen.* BELLYSONG *makes a motion as if to kill a roach. Continues conversation.*]

BELLYSONG.   No, but I really love Nemesis, Pariah.

PARIAH.   [*absently*] Hmmm.

BELLYSONG.   You don't believe that?

PARIAH.   I can believe anything.

BELLYSONG.   Well, she just doesn't understand me, that's all. She's a good woman. God knows, but she just doesn't understand me. I've got a question for you though, Pariah.

PARIAH.   What?

BELLYSONG.   Is it possible . . . [*pause*] How shall I put this? Is it possible for a man to have sex regularly, without going out of his mind in the process? I mean, obviously marriage is an arrangement for the continual access of sex, right? Yet you still have each other's pains and moods to deal with. If you chase girls around, it requires loss of energy, compromise of soul, and possible end of sanity. Prostitution is uncertain. What can a reasonable good man do?

PARIAH.   Pray. I've got a better question for you. How can a man do *anything* in this world without giving up his mind?

BELLYSONG.   Hmm. You're right. [*there's a long silence*] You know, Pariah . . . I sometimes become very frightened.

PARIAH. Why?

BELLYSONG. I don't know. I . . . don't. I think I've always been in a state of preparation. You know, always getting ready for something. I mean . . . I always expect it to be coming; but it's not. This is it. Nemesis, you, Bo-Simon, Miss Nancy, you're all it. You're my life. I'm forty-seven now and it's all over. Whatever I was waiting for is here. I was drafted, you know. The war was going on. I don't remember the war, just a few scenes, a few people. And then it was over and I was out, and it . . . all doesn't seem real. Do you understand what I mean?

PARIAH. I understand.

BELLYSONG. I mean, I just don't believe my whole life . . . it's unreal. It never began. [*stands up*] I mean . . . it's a farce. This is *it*.

PARIAH. Oh well . . . you know. No one's moving anywhere. We're all just looking at each other through frosted glass. Actually, we're all standing perfectly still, doing tiny things with our hands.

BELLYSONG. You're young.

PARIAH. You're older.

BELLYSONG. You're a poet.

PARIAH. You're an artisan.

BELLYSONG. I'm glad you're back.

PARIAH. I'm glad you're glad.

BELLYSONG. You've got to read me some of your new stuff.

PARIAH.   I've got to write some new stuff for you to read.

BELLYSONG.   What the hell did you do in Europe?

PARIAH.   I arrived, and then a lot of time happened, and then I left. Played the young man of delicate sensibility among merchants. Ate, went to the toilet, dressed, that's all.

BELLYSONG.   Oh. [*They laugh.*] Well, it could be worse, I guess.

PARIAH.   [*pause*] If it could, Bellysong, it would be. [*They laugh again.*] Did you ever feel as if you were in a painting?

BELLYSONG.   Yeah. An unfinished one.

PARIAH.   In the beginning the Lord made the heaven and the earth . . . and then he got bored. [*They dance a small minuet.*]

[*darkness*]

SCENE FIVE

[PARIAH ANON's *soliloquy. The scene is the Lower East Side,* PARIAH *is waiting for* ANNE.]

PARIAH.   Here I am again on the Lower East Side. [*long pause*] What the fuck am I doing back on the Lower East Side? The same apartment houses; the same places I used to get drunk at; the same gutters I used to throw up in. I thought all of this was over. Europe should have worked, I had it totally in my hands.

It's like waking up from a dream back into a nightmare. [*long pause*] Pity I blew England, I would have fitted so well in a Rolls Royce. The labor government is now, I would of had to settle for a Bentley. That's all right though. I'd of fit well in a Bentley too. [*does a panto-mime of sitting in a chauffeured car*] Um, to Chelsea, John, and on the way do stop at that street corner and pick up that little girl in the yellow mini. There's a good fellow. [*pause*] Come along dear, yes, you honey, we're on our way to the palace.

Must remember to borrow a few dollars from Anne. Get a few clean rags on my ass for a change until I can get back on welfare. I'm going to have to either marry that girl or become a junkie. [*pauses*] Hell no, if I marry her, I will become a junkie, her mind is too damn diabolical, she'd probably drive me to it. Couldn't get away very much with her around.

Jesus, I've got to get wealthy, there's no other way to make it. And I better do it soon or it won't do me any damn good. I'm going to have a hernia by the time I'm thirty, probably have ulcers too.

I could just see myself, being wheeled through Washington Square, multitudes of hot creaming women laying about, Anne bending down and whispering in my ear, don't excite yourself, dear, you know that's not good for you, remember what the doctor said. [*long pause*] If only her father would hurry up and die, I'd marry her in a second. He's looking healthier than ever these days though. Ever since he got that new law office . . . That paunch of his though, you never can tell, could go in a minute. Much too many after hour cocktails. [*looks around him*] Hell, I've got to get the fuck out of this place before I die. [*screams out suddenly*] Let me out of here, Goddammit. The Puerto Ricans playing the same boring music. The Ukrainians out planning new pogroms. Let me out of here, you people have ceased to be amusing. You people are either filthy or ignorant, [*pause*] usually both. I don't belong here, dammit, I deserve better than this. [*pause*] Come on now, get yourself together, Pariah, can't go around screaming on the good little people's street corner. They put your little rump away in odd little places with wire partitions and people peering in on you and taking notes in strange little notebooks. Don't want that, do we? Remember Humpty Dumpty, all the king's horses, and all the king's men, etc. And I'm a hell of a lot blacker than he ever was.

[*enter* BELLYSONG *to announce the entrance of* ANNE]

SCENE SIX

[PARIAH ANON *is seated on a park bench. A portion of Bach's* Orgelbuchlein *music is heard at the beginning of this scene, which slowly fades out upon the entrance of* ANNE. ANNE *is a young Jewess (about twenty-six) from the Bronx. She is not afflicted with an accent. She is a very sensible, yet kind girl with a general love for Pariah which transcends* soi-disant *liberalism. (She's known him too long for that. It is readily apparent that the relationship has existed for at least four years.)*
PARIAH *sitting sartorial, a pensive para-bored look on his face.*]

ANNE. [*walking slowly up to him*] You bastard!

PARIAH. Hello, love. Was just sitting here thinking of growing a mustache or perhaps a beard. Something to connote a bit of distinction.

ANNE. You filthy . . . bastard.

PARIAH. Hmmm, you know you really possess very little variety?

ANNE. How could you?

PARIAH. How could I what, may I ask?

ANNE. How could you have written my father for money?

PARIAH. Very simple, really. I took my right hand, being dextrous, positioned a pen within, and then by a quaint digital process, I . . .

ANNE. [*produces letter; begins to read*] London, September fifth. Dear Dad . . .

PARIAH. I thought it best to employ the familiar in "matters of supplication."

ANNE. [*rereads*] Dear Dad: Do hope this letter does not find you in dispirit.

Have suffered much sea-change here in this Roman city. At present, my fiscal situation is elemental. My keeper, here in this lazar house, has threatened me with imprisonment. All of which is too complexed and vulgar to go into now. I do, however, need the sum of $550 (five hundred and fifty dollars) to accomplish a safe remove from these quarters. Doubtless, you're glad to hear that I am alive and well in a foreign country. I do very much await your epistle. Hoping all is well with Mrs. Finklestein and young Jacob.

Yours in distress,
Pariah

> P.S. If unfortunately for some reason I do not hear from you, I shall probably have no recourse but to get word to Anne, who as you well know, would probably leap over to this unnatural country to save my body from perishment. Do forgive me. Be well.

PARIAH. Hmmm.

ANNE. How could you?

PARIAH. It was necessary. One does what's necessary. You wouldn't have me sell my body, would you?

ANNE. You could have worked.

PARIAH. Impossible. No jobs. They all come *here* to work, re-member?

ANNE. What makes you think my father owes you a living?

PARIAH. Well, a simple pre-Platonic logic. He has, I do not.

ANNE. He worked long and hard for his money.

PARIAH. Yes, but think of all the people he's wronged on the way. I'm merely his penance. He'll be able to die free, and go straight to Heaven. He does believe in Heaven, doesn't he?

ANNE. Oh, that's your role in life. To see that people go to Heaven, eh?

PARIAH. I'll tell you, Anne, you see it's really very simple. There was a great mistake made at my birth.

ANNE. Illegitimacy.

PARIAH. Besides that, I should have been born White Anglo-Saxon Protestant. And float through my life with all the Protestant fantasies. Sit up crossed-legged at Harvard or Princeton; play at the humanities, you know.

Pariah Anon set loose at Radcliffe, or Wellesley, or the yard at Smith. Sip port in some restaurant with sawdust floors. Discourse at length on why Da Vinci wrote Greek backwards.

Or at least Jewish, with access to community, family, and fraternity. Be given a year's rent for a wedding present. Be ambitious; what was your high school average again, ninety-six or something?

ANNE. Ninety-eight point six. [smiling]

PARIAH. I knew it was something offensive like that. I would even settle to have been born part of the Black Bourgeoisie. Live in the West Village, sandled and detached. Perfect: a eunuchoidal walk. Be proceeded by two slender greyhounds, wherever I go. Develop an interest in opera or something. Sit in parks, be shat upon by domestic birds, talk at length to young mothers pushing prams. Life of leisure, that.

ANNE. Be serious for a change. What are you going to do about your life?

PARIAH. Well, I was thinking of waiting until your father quit this mortal coil. Live off the pretty inheritance.

ANNE. If my father does die, he won't leave me a cent as long as I am still seeing you. He's made that clear.

PARIAH. Yes, somehow I'm not beloved by him. Listen, I have a lot of respect and sympathy for your father; after all it's not easy being a lawyer and making sure your guilty clients get away with it. And—well, you know—

it wasn't that long ago that he was sitting and cheering Paul Robeson. Of course, he told me he saw *Othello*, everyone in the world apparently saw *Othello*. And your dear old dad was blacklisted when he was working with the theater. What's the Brechtian line about "eating one's lunch between wars." [*sighs*] And now after all that struggle his son is running in the East Village, his hair longer than yours. His daughter who he lavished all his hopes upon falls in love with a worthless Negro poet, without connections, without ambition, and who has no intention of changing. Life is sometimes very cruel.

ANNE. All right, stop patting yourself on the back. What happened in England?

PARIAH. Well, you know the British no longer have an empire to play with, so they play with themselves now. There are men in this world who are not wholly kind. Naughty men (mostly white: heh heh) who roll their little hands into tight fists. Men who want to bruise my small body for some reason. And unfortunately these unkind men seem always to be in power, or places of power. [*He pauses to think of his words. Turns to audience in such a way that it's a direct confrontation.*] And these men always seem to be behind smooth desks [*makes figure of desk with his hands*] with people about them—usually dwarfs—holding cross-staves. Always in badly lit airless rooms. And to these men, I say, I say . . . gentlemen, it's really, really not nice at all what you're doing, and I wag the pointed finger, but somehow strangely . . . it doesn't seem to do any good. Yet, apparently, I offend these people, Anne.

ANNE. You could get somewhere with your poetry, at least make a little money from some readings.

PARIAH. I don't read in public. I'm not an entertainer. I'm a poet. Always the conflict of the public and the private. It's bad enough that one has to publish.

ANNE. You haven't been published, remember.

PARIAH. Hmm. Did I tell you about the time Langston Hughes read my poetry?

ANNE. About a million times.

PARIAH. Well, he was quite taken with it. Said I'd make it. That's no little thing, you know.

ANNE. Oh, what's the use.

PARIAH. [stands and begins to pace back and forth humorously, with his hands behind him, as though ice-skating] But Europe was interesting.

ANNE. Was it?

PARIAH. Had to mount stairs and escalators slowly, lest someone notice the hole in my ragged pants. Once my member came out, very disconcerting. A little girl told her mommy: "Mommy, Mommy, look at that awful Negro with his thing hanging out." "Pay no attention to him, Clarissa; he's just foul."

ANNE. [laughing] Really?

PARIAH. Took it all in my stride and put it back in closed quarters.

ANNE. Thursday's your birthday.

PARIAH. I feared you'd forgotten.

ANNE.   What are you planning on doing?

PARIAH.   Staying at home and reading my verse aloud to myself. [*begins to read out in Nero-like fashion*] Oh . . . sun . . . oh . . . sea . . .

ANNE.   Oh shit.

PARIAH.   You know you have a singular dislike of art. Shows indelicacy of breeding, I suspect.

ANNE.   I like you. Do I also have to like art?

PARIAH.   Point.

[*sits down.*]

ANNE.   What's going to become of you?

PARIAH.   I'm going to fail, of course. My life's an experiment that can't possibly work. I want to leave the world the way I came in it: innocent. You can't do that. Or maybe some wealthy Black millionaire—one whose ancestors made money from slavery or something—will feel a twinge of guilt and leave me a small fortune to write beautiful verse. Maybe he likes my art-for-art's-sake attitude. Support gratuitous art, etc.

ANNE.   Ha ha. [*mockingly*]

PARIAH.   Well, maybe . . . I'll get a nice liberated Afro-American girl, you know, who goes to an analyst twice a week, with a tidy account in the Washington Carver Bank.

ANNE.   What do you want to do Thursday?

PARIAH.   Spend the day in bed with you, of course. What the hell else?

ANNE. Okay. I'll take the day off. [*sighs*] I hope you aren't planning any more trips to Europe soon.

PARIAH. I can't. I can't go anywhere. I'm a freak traveling among the uncircumcised. No place to go at all, love. No place. Except beneath the earth, to grow weeds and a bit of concrete on top for some old woman to measure distance by.

[*darkness*]

SCENE SEVEN

[BELLYSONG *is in a bar.*]

FELLOW IN CROWD. Give us a speech, Bellysong. Give us a speech. [*He staggers to his feet, holds on to a chair and then stands on it, holding bottle in right hand like a scepter.*]

BELLYSONG. All right, all right. I'm going . . . I'm going to . . . extemporize on a theme. The theme . . .

CHORUS. Yeah, yeah, go on, Bellysong.

BELLYSONG. [*continuing*] The theme shall be, "Why do the bastards survive?" You see, when I was young, see, and when I was young before I was old, I had a million ideas, see. And they had kicked my behind in the South, so I came North.
And I wore my shirt open then.
(Didn't wear a coat in winter.)

And like I said I had a million ideas
But when I came to New York I met people who had
twenty million ideas.
And these people said: "Well, fella, you're an artist, I
see. I like the way you sculpt. You got a mind, too.
You've read a lot, oh?" Well, yeah, I read . . . I've done
a lot of reading. Well, you see, all these people doing
all these things. Claude McKay running around in Russia,
writing poetry.
And DuBois talking and stuff.
And there was Robeson and Richard Wright.
"The times are changing, fella, see."
Yeah, I see.
So I ran around in the Village. (You could eat then.)
Carried portfolios of sketches.
Talked with all those good free people . . . about being
good and free.
Talked about psychology. That was a big thing then.
And proletariat art. Stuff like Delacroix's French paint-
ings. People breaking chains.
Dancing in Union Square. Wow.
Just great . . . just marvelous.
Russia was going to do all sorts of great things. Lead
the way.
Fellows on horseback. Big tartars, virile, healthy. Sitting
around, talking about Prokofiev's music.
Waiting . . . waiting.
Getting together every now and then to exchange
fantasies.
All the gay heroes from the Abraham Lincoln Brigade.
And the days went on and the nights went. But that's
not what I wanted to say.

CHORUS.   What is it you want to say, Bellysong?
What is it?

BELLYSONG.   To say . . . to say that I can't. To say that the people that I met that I thought I knew but didn't know as I thought I knew, the people who I thought . . . the people who said, "Yes, it will be something. It will be something else." The people who moved in and out between my life in their peculiar styles of living. The others who moved through neon lights. Fabulous dazzling people.

The people who held out hands or didn't . . . All of us running, but really only sitting. The others who maybe did want to do something good. Really did mean to do something. The people who really wanted but didn't know . . .

The nothing which we waited on yesterday, waiting by the door, or in the street.

The nothing, which did in fact not come, will be the nothing which will not come tomorrow.

And always there will be just enough food. Just enough dust. Just enough of each other to make us content enough to wait. You see . . .

CHORUS. No.

BELLYSONG. I mean it's just a dance we do.

CHORUS. A dance?

BELLYSONG. A little dance.

CHORUS. A blind man.

BELLYSONG. A blind man. And I feel like I'm made out of straw.

[*darkness*]

SCENE EIGHT

[MISS NANCY RILEY'S *morning prayer*]

MISS NANCY. [*goes to front of stage and does pantomime of opening window*] Oh my, oh my, look at that sun out there. Just where it was yesterday. It's so nice to find things where you left them. It makes you think things are going [*pause*] smoothly. That's so pleasant.

Lord, please, let Bellysong come by today. I really shouldn't see him anymore. But I've done lots of things I shouldn't already. One more ain't going to hurt too much. [*turns to go, then pauses and turns back*] Well, keep everything [*pause*] going.

[*exit*]

SCENE NINE

[NANCY RILEY *at the grave of her husband.* BELLYSONG JONES *announces the scene.*]

BELLYSONG. Miss Nancy Riley, widow of four years, visits the grave of her husband Albert.

[NANCY RILEY *enters stage and kneels down before a cardboard box with a cross stuck in on top.*]

MISS NANCY. Hello Albert, it's very bright today. Lots of sunshine. [*pause*] I brought you some crackers. [*takes out a box of crackers, breaks them up and scatters them on grave*] I thought maybe you're a little hungry. My goodness, it's so peaceful here, you're real close to Mr. Perkins. [*looks around as though looking at the other grave*] Guess you two have a lot to talk about these days. You know, Albert, they're still sending your *Reader's Digest* to the house, I kept up the subscription. I tried to tell them that you're [*pause*] not with us any longer, but they keep sending them in your name.

[*A very tired looking* NEGRO MAN *comes up to* NANCY RILEY *at this point.*]

MAN. Excuse me, but I seem to be lost. I was just visiting my wife, she's over there at site 287 you know. Do you know the quickest way out of here.

MISS NANCY. Oh certainly, just follow that path till you come to the tomb with a young boy seated holding a book.

MAN. Oh yeah, I remember that one.

MISS NANCY. Then turn right until you come to the grave of the um . . . well, you'll recognize it, a grave with red flowers and white and yellow that make the words: "To my dearest Mother."

MAN. To my dearest mother, ah hah—all right.

MISS NANCY. Then go straight.

MAN. Thank you very much, I always get lost in this place.

MISS NANCY. My pleasure. [*turns back to her husband's grave*] Excuse me, Albert, I was interrupted. [*pause*] The deacon wants me to marry him. [*pause*] I told him I didn't know, I'd have to think about it. I don't know if I want to get married no more. [*pause*] I came over the bridge today. I saw one of those Hudson Day Liners go by, you know? It was all filled with people in bright hats, holding picnic lunches and stuff. We did that once, remember? [*long pause*] I think we were happy then.

[*darkness*]

SCENE TEN

[*Home of* NANCY RILEY. *She is sitting, sipping coffee. She affects total gentility. She speaks in a sparrow-like voice.* BELLYSONG *knocks.*]

MISS NANCY. Who is it?

BELLYSONG. It's Bellysong Jones, Miss Nancy.

[MISS NANCY *opens door.*]

MISS NANCY. Bellysong, well, come in. I thought you said that . . .

BELLYSONG. Yes, I know what I said. I just want to play the piano. [*He walks over to the piano, falls down in seat, takes his thickish hands, and clumsily begins to play Bach's "Sleepers Awake." She, a woman of forty-five, thick-bodied though still well-built, sits on the edge of her chair watching in awe. He plays three times until he successfully gets through the better part of it. He looks at his hands laughing.*] You know, everything I touch turns to crap, pure moist turd. My wife, on the other hand, keeps going, always ready to climb the wall all over again. She can be pleased with a political revolution. She thinks that a political revolution means good people taking over from the bad. When I say freedom she thinks about being able to use any outhouse you want to. Things are indeed very simple for my darling wife.

MISS NANCY.   Bellysong, I'm not sure I understand what you mean either.

BELLYSONG.   Doubtless, beloved, doubtless. Come here. Let me feel that amazing southern-fried body of yours.

MISS NANCY.   Hee-hee, look now, I got a fiancé who wants to marry me. I shouldn't be fooling around with a married man.

BELLYSONG.   You're not, my dear. You're fooling around with the most unmarried man in the world. [*He takes her and leads her into the darkened room. She mutters something and the sound of door shutting is heard.*]

SCENE ELEVEN

[*At the home of* BELLYSONG, NEMESIS *retires to bed with a drink of gin and a hot water bag.*]

NEMESIS.   Lord, I don't know why I married, when I was twenty and had those flowers on me all over me. All those jazz singers would look at me when I walked and all those jokes about the "Carolina Girl" and they all high as

Georgia pines, and I could bull-jive them for a dress or a coat or anything I wanted and now . . . But mama told me she had a vision that I shouldn't marry him cause she said I was in a forest and this animal was chasing me and my feet were paralyzed, just like when I was pregnant with my first baby and I couldn't walk. Thank God he died. Lord, you know best, because he didn't even come to Harlem Hospital to see me or the baby cause he was drunk, frightened to be a man always running, frightened of telephones, frightened of his name, frightened of responsibility, and don't let anything happen to Alfred, please Lord, it was worth it to have a son to hear him peeing in the bathroom or watching him try to grow a beard because my father had one but such a gentle voice a gentleman that's why I loved him stranger than all the rest calling me Miss Nemesis and I could see he was shy but they're all the same and those must have been tears in mama's eyes.

SCENE TWELVE

[BELLYSONG *advances to the center of the stage and creates the setting.*]

BELLYSONG. The home of Mr. Solomon and Rebecca Finklestein. In the walls are two reproductions of Chagall's paintings. One small genuine Pollack. The *Jewish Encyclopedia*, unopened. [*pause*] A biography of Ben-Gurion, Joyce's *Ulysses*, [*pause*] once opened. A volume of Bialick's poetry. A million or so issues of *Commentary*. Anne takes Pariah home to pick up things [*pause*] money.

[ANNE *and* PARIAH *enter doorway;* MRS. FINKLE-
STEIN *is sitting on sofa, speaking and laughing
into phone. She sees* PARIAH *and quickly ends
conversation.* ANNE *just walks across stage as if
going to her room.*]

MRS. FINKLESTEIN.   [*staring at* PARIAH, *calls out frantically*] Sol!
Sol!

PARIAH.   [*in choir-like voice*] Hello, Mrs. Finklestein.

MRS. FINKLESTEIN.   Sol!

SOL.   [*enters wearing Japanese bathrobe, obviously he's been
bathing*] For Christ's sake, can't I even take a bath in
peace? [*sees* PARIAH] No, you wouldn't have the nerve.

PARIAH.   Hi there, just got back. [*There is a long silence.*] Anne
just wanted to pick up a few things.

SOL.   Anne, get this black bastard out of my house!

PARIAH.   I do wish you wouldn't say that.

ANNE.   [*coming back to living room*] What's the hysteria about?

SOL.   What's the hysteria about? "What's the hysteria," she says.
How could you have the nerve to bring him here?

ANNE.   Now, daddy, you agreed to be liberal.

SOL.   Liberal, Goddammit, I don't mind if you go out with a
Negro. If you really wanted to, you could even marry a
Negro. But Christ Jesus, not him.

PARIAH.   Lovely robe, Mr. Finklestein.

MRS. FINKLESTEIN.   Sol, please, fix me a drink.

SOL.   [*nervously going to bar*] What kind do you want, dear?

MRS. FINKLESTEIN.   A large one, Sol.

ANNE.   Listen, I just want to get a few things. We'll be out of here fast.

SOL.   [*spilling drink*] You're not leaving with him. That's the last straw. Pariah, get out now.

PARIAH.   Sir, I realize that in the past I've done certain imprudent things, however—

SOL.   Imprudent? Get out!

ANNE.   Daddy, I know about the letter from Europe. But he promised he won't do anything like that again.

MRS. FINKLESTEIN.   Sol, the drink.

SOL.   How much do I have to do for this bastard, give him my life? When he got in a fight with those three Italian boys—

ANNE.   What three boys?

PARIAH.   Oh, you remember those three guys who said those unfortunate things to me. They were the worse for it.

SOL.   So gorilla here throws them through a plate-glass window. One guy gets his collarbone broken. I have to defend him. Why doesn't he go in the ring and make some damn money?

ANNE.   Well, Daddy, he was provoked.

MRS. FINKLESTEIN. [*on sofa, grasping hair*] Sol!

SOL. And what about the time he stole that typewriter from the pawnshop window?

PARIAH. What's a writer without a typewriter?

SOL. And then you sold it, you bastard.

PARIAH. What's a writer without food?

SOL. He's always in trouble and when he gets caught, who do they come to? Me, that's who.

ANNE. I'm getting my things. [*walks offstage*]

SOL. [*craftily*] Listen, Pariah, if it's money you want—

PARIAH. Well, as a matter of fact—

ANNE. [*entering again*] Pariah!

PARIAH. All right, all right, I didn't accept. [ANNE *leaves again.*]

SOL. [*placatingly*] Pariah, what is it you want?

PARIAH. Not much, really.

SOL. You don't want to hurt Anne, do you?

PARIAH. No, I don't want to hurt her.

SOL. Then the kindest thing that you can do for her is to leave her alone.

PARIAH. Oh, I can't leave her now.

SOL *and* MOTHER. [*in unison*] Why?

PARIAH.   Oh, because I've gotten used to her.

SOL.   Have you ever thought of anyone besides yourself?

PARIAH.   Not that I remember, no.

ANNE.   [*reentering*] All right, I think I have all I need. I'll be back next week, everybody.

MRS. FINKLESTEIN.   All right, Anne, you can leave with him if you want to.

ANNE.   Thank you, Mom, I knew that—

MRS. FINKLESTEIN.   You can leave, [*pause*] and I'll just jump right out that window.

ANNE.   Oh, Mom!

SOL.   What I want to know is what the hell you want Anne for. You're not ugly, you could get any damn girl you want to.

ANNE.   Daddy, how could you?

PARIAH.   Well . . .

SOL.   Yeah, I know, you're used to her. You can get used to somebody else for God's sake.

PARIAH.   Well, you see . . . Dad?

SOL.   Don't call me Dad, I had nothing to do with your birth.

PARIAH.   You see, it's like this. I've got art covered, she has everything else covered.

ANNE.   A Master's in Economics and one in Sociology.

SOL.   I know what degrees you have. I'm the one who paid for your education, remember? And I'm still paying.

PARIAH.   So I figured together we could take the world.

ANNE.   Let's go, Pariah.

SOL.   [*paternally*] Pariah, don't get her pregnant, eh?

PARIAH.   Oh, I won't. If I do, I'll marry her.

SOL.   No, don't marry her, please. Just send her home.

PARIAH.   Wouldn't you like a nice curly-headed grandson? Mixed marriages make such lovely children.

SOL.   Hell no, her hair is kinky enough as it is.

ANNE.   Dad?

PARIAH.   [*looking at* ANNE'*s hair*] True.

SOL.   Go on, get out of here.

MRS. FINKLESTEIN.   Sol.

[ANNE *kisses her father and turns to exit.*]

PARIAH.   Well, [*pause*] see you around.

SOL.   Undoubtedly, one baby and I'll kill you. [*They leave.*]

MRS. FINKLESTEIN.   Sol, how could you let her leave with that . . . that . . .

SOL.   Black bastard.

MRS. FINKLESTEIN. Black bastard.

SOL. What could we do, lock her in her room? Make her wear a chastity belt? There isn't a damn thing we can do.

MRS. FINKLESTEIN. Sol, call my analyst.

SOL. Which one?

MRS. FINKLESTEIN. Dr. Feldman. And bring me my yellow pills.

SOL. [*dials phone*] Hello, is Dr. Feldman in? What? He's where? How can an analyst go on vacation for God's sake?

[*darkness*]

SCENE THIRTEEN

[BELLYSONG JONES *walks across stage, smoking cigar. Announces next scene, the East Village apartment of* PARIAH ANON.]

BELLYSONG. The East Village apartment of Pariah Anon. The East Village is a place uncommonly filled with layabouts and cutpurses. The guilty looking and the besotted.

[ANNE *and* PARIAH *in bedroom.* ANNE *is laying in bed working on* Times' *crossword puzzle. On the left wall is a large photograph of the electric chair at Sing Sing.* PARIAH *is seated half-naked on the floor. He has his hands entwined about himself, in a position much like one of a straight-*

jacket. At the head of the bed BELLYSONG *and*
NEMESIS *stand silent holding sprig leaves or
banners in the sign of fertility. They are dressed
in purple.*]

ANNE.　Pariah, what are you doing sitting on the floor like that,
with your arms wrapped around you?

PARIAH.　I'm decomposing.

ANNE.　Just narcissism, that's all. You are about the weirdest. . . .
And why don't you take that photograph of the electric
chair down. I swear it's morbid.

PARIAH.　Gives one a sense of perspective.

ANNE.　Gives me a sense of the chills. [*long silence; she goes back
to puzzle*] A six-letter word meaning a state of bliss,
Pariah?

PARIAH.　A what?

ANNE.　A six-letter word meaning a state of bliss.

PARIAH.　I don't know. I don't think like *The New York Times*.

ANNE.　[*mimicking him*] I don't think like *The New York Times*.
[*back to normal voice*] So smug. So superior. Buddha in
the corner. What the hell do you have to be so smug
about? You think you have a great secret?

PARIAH.　I think I have nothing.

ANNE.　Well, you have something but nothing to be smug about,
that's all. [*returns to puzzle*] I was thinking of quitting
social work. I can't stand it anymore.

PARIAH.   Oh, then you should quit.

ANNE.   It's too futile. My heart was in the right place at first. I could picture long rows of penitents in white robes, you know.

PARIAH.   Could you?

ANNE.   Yeah, and stand there holding bandages and little flasks of water.

PARIAH.   That's before you change the water to wine.

ANNE.   Right, right. Think I'll go back into psychology. Pariah . . . do you think people have children for any other reason than vanity?

PARIAH.   No.

ANNE.   [*returning to puzzle*] Who was Agamemnon's brother?

PARIAH.   The brother of Agamemnon.

ANNE.   Thank you, Mr. Philosopher. All Xs are Ys except when they aren't.

PARIAH.   Yeah . . . except when they aren't.

ANNE.   Right, except when they aren't. Smug, so smug. He knows it all.

[PARIAH *crawls over to the bed on all fours.*]

PARIAH.   [*whispers*] We're all building a house.

ANNE.   Who?

PARIAH.   Everyone.

ANNE. What house?

PARIAH. An awkward one.

ANNE. You too.

PARIAH. Me too.

ANNE. Is that your great secret?

PARIAH. That's my only secret, so I guess it's my great one.

ANNE. And who's in it?

PARIAH. No one. Everyone. But they don't know.

ANNE. Don't know what?

PARIAH. That they're building.

ANNE. But you, Pariah Anon, know.

PARIAH. Yes, but I don't know why.

ANNE. You don't know why.

PARIAH. I don't know if there is a why.

ANNE. People are strange.

PARIAH. Ssh . . . quiet.

ANNE. Why?

PARIAH. I'm listening to the sound of my blood corpuscles through my body.

ANNE. Blood corpuscles.

PARIAH. It's a race.

ANNE. It's a race riot.

PARIAH. Folk wit.

ANNE. [*placing her ear near his chest*] I don't hear anything.

PARIAH. As long as you're down there, why don't you . . .

ANNE. [*slapping his chest coyly, and turning back to her puzzle, as he laughs*] Women are funny.

PARIAH. Ha ha. [*dryly*]

ANNE. No, really. Walking around with holes in the middle. Always peeing on ourselves. They lack a center.

PARIAH. Do they?

ANNE. They can't stand straight.

PARIAH. [*his eyes closed*] Pictures.

ANNE. What?

PARIAH. Pictures in my brain. Oh . . . wait; I don't like that one.

ANNE. What do you see?

PARIAH. A man with a humped back and pocked face just entered a building. He came in by a revolving door.

ANNE. [*passing her hand over his face*] And now?

PARIAH. It's gone. Now I see a sponge with feet. He just excused himself to go to the toilet. [*lights dim*] Come a little closer . . . there . . .

ANNE. And now . . . ?

PARIAH. I like it . . . here. Grassy. It's snowing. No heat. [*laughs*] It's the sea . . . flooding . . . Ah . . .

[*darkness*]

SCENE FOURTEEN

[*All characters are in Brooks Brothers suits. Darkness. A light suddenly appears showing* BELLYSONG *walking about in wonder. Second light shows* PARIAH. *He too is stumbling. They do not see each other. They eventually bump into one another.*]

PARIAH. Bellysong? But how did I . . .

[*The whole stage suddenly becomes flooded with light.*]

BELLYSONG. I don't know . . . I think . . . yes, we're finally here . . . but I don't remember dying.

PARIAH. You mean . . . dear God, at last, you bastard. Now I can confront you, now for all the ages. Where is he, where is God? [*shouts*] Come out, come out, we're equal now, now for all the stench of the ages.

[*A group of angels walks across the stage. They*

*speak one with another and do not appear to
notice* BELLYSONG *and* PARIAH.]

PARIAH.   You there! Where is he?

BELLYSONG.   No need to yell now, Pariah.

ONE OF THE ANGELS.   [*turning to* PARIAH] I say, there must be
some mistake, there was no one expected today.

PARIAH.   Mistake? I am Pariah Anon, the formless son of a
diseased race, who, after much sea-change and tumult,
am here to see the Lord, your God.

BELLYSONG.   You're in fine voice, Pariah.

THE ANGELS.   He does sound bitter, doesn't he?

FIRST ANGEL.   Yes. Well, it's only because he's a new arrival.
Pretty skin though, hasn't he? Ah, listen fellow, you see,
I don't quite know how to say this but, ah well, you
see, I believe you weren't supposed to come yet . . . ah
. . . you see, I'm first in command and there are three
due from a military encounter (bad business that encounter, a thousand killed there. Apparently the General
failed in bed with some women or other, and ordered a
ridiculous attack), however, they're not due until the
day after tomorrow.

PARIAH.   The bastard. I want to see him now. I want to spit in
his face.

FIRST ANGEL.   Spit in his . . . I say, look, it's quite impossible.
Please, why don't you just . . .

VOICE FROM WINGS.   Thomas, what is all that noise?

164   THE MUMMER'S PLAY

FIRST ANGEL. [*whispers*] Oh goodness, we're going to catch it now. [*louder*] Ah . . . nothing sir, just a small mix-up as it were.

[*Old bent man comes limping out in spotted nightshirt.*]

ST. PETER. What's that you say, Thomas? By the way, where's Nietzche? My chamber pot needs emptying. Now who are these two?

BELLYSONG. I am Demosthenes Bellysong Jones, and my young friend here is . . .

PARIAH. No, Bellysong, let me introduce myself to The Very Lord God of Hosts. I am Pariah Anon.

ST. PETER. Would you like a piece of candy? Very good I find.

PARIAH. [*infuriated*] No, damn you. You won't escape now.

ST. PETER. Escape? Indeed.

BELLYSONG. Pariah, I don't think that he . . .

PARIAH. I know it's here, I'd only written it yesterday. It was in Nemesis's brown wrapping paper . . . a poem . . . [*fumbles through pockets*] it must be here. Ah yes . . . [*finds it, opens it, and begins reading*]

The pity is that man is sudden
the terror is that man will cease
arked between the perfect and the perfect
we dash our brains in sad abuse.
Because you are the belly's rumble
the ash-taste from the mouth of death,

because you are the dark summoner
that puts us in the night of time,
you common us with age-old hatreds,
you leave us voiceless as the Nazarène [*his voice breaks.*]

BELLYSONG.   Don't stop my boy, it's a very good poem.

THE ANGELS.   Yes, very beautiful, isn't it? And so sad, so mortally
sad.

ST. PETER.   Are you sure you wouldn't like a candy? An orange
then? It's very comforting to the bowels you know.

PARIAH.   [*recovering his voice, begins again*]
The pity is that man is sudden
thorny seed of a spent confusion.
And you the God-dark of the sky . . .

ST. PETER.   [*breaking in*] Please, please. I would like to hear
your poem. It's a very good poem as poems go, I mean,
it doesn't offend the ear. But you see, I'm not him.

PARIAH.   Not him?

ST. PETER.   No, you see I'm the one they call Peter, ah . . .
Saint Peter as it were, and I'm only . . . ah, Nietzche
you rascal, come here. [*Another old man comes from
stage left. He wears a white shiny suit and has a thick
white mustache.*] Nietzche, you know you forgot the
chamber pot again this morning.

NIETZCHE.   Oh, forgive me, I meant . . . I was . . . that is,
I must have forgotten. I'll see to it straightaway.
You know . . . I . . . meant to . . . I . . . because
. . . I'll see to it straightaway.

ST. PETER. Please do, Nietzche, and . . . in the future . . .
Would you like some candy, Nietzche?

NIETZCHE. Candy? Yes, I would like a candy. That would be
very pleasant. [*takes candy from outstretched hand of*
ST. PETER]

ST. PETER. They give a sweet taste to the mouth.

NIETZCHE. [*sucking mechanically*] Yes . . . a very sweet taste.

ST. PETER. Please, now don't forget the pot.

[*exit* NIETZCHE]

ST. PETER. Yes, now what was I saying . . . oh yes, no, no,
I'm not he. I'm simply Peter.

PARIAH. Well, where is he?

ST. PETER. He's up in the chambers, I suspect. That's where he
usually stays these days. He's not much given to talk
of late.

PARIAH. Not much given to talk of late? The bastard fashions
himself a world and lets the vipers prosper. He slays
nations without mercy, he takes the holiest and spits on
them for their generations, and you tell me that he's
not much given to talk of late? What is his reason for
this mess?

ST. PETER. Reason? There was a reason once . . . but I forget.
I think he said . . . when he first made me, I was a
slender boy made without fault, but then he soon de-
formed me and made me into an old man because he
said I would have better understanding then . . . I believe it was because he was lonely.

PARIAH. Lonely. Yes, of course.

ST. PETER. But we haven't *done* anything. He merely organized a world, and He thought it would be a little more interesting if there were more types, and then . . . or was it that curse? No . . . no . . . I believe it was only accidental . . . I'm not very certain anymore. Anyway, they all die and we bring the most interesting here.

PARIAH. Like Nietzche, who empties your chamber pot?

ST. PETER. Yes, well, you see it gives him a feeling of power and some usefulness, like your poems.

PARIAH. My poems? All directed to an old man with bad bowels. [*tears up poem*]

BELLYSONG. No, Pariah, don't!

ST. PETER. Oh, I'm so very tired. A little sleep now. Thomas, attend these two for me, I'm overweary.

[*starts to walk off, then stops, ponders and turns around*]

ST. PETER. Wait, there was something I told that other poet some time ago. Yes, you have a function.

PARIAH. A function, old man?

ST. PETER. Yes, to teach them grace, a way of moving in life. To give them . . . to give them a remembrance, a careful remembrance of things they've never known and are therefore familiar. [*walks away muttering*] . . . of things they've never known . . . and are therefore familiar . . . Nietzche, where are you?

THOMAS. Well, Mr. Anon, since you're going to be with us from now on, perhaps you'll lead a group of the angels in a poetry seminar? Now, we can arrange for a few hours a day, whatever is convenient for you. You know, I write a few verses myself sometimes. Of course, I don't consider myself a poet, ah . . . as it were, but . . .

SCENE FIFTEEN

[BELLYSONG *returns home. It is about three-thirty* A.M. *He stumbles again into kitchen.*]

VOICE FROM INSIDE. Is that you, Bellysong?

BELLYSONG. [*too tired to argue*] Yeah, it's me. It's me. [*He sits down at table, takes out morning paper, drinks coffee.*] Well, it's almost morning. It's not too bad now. [*kills roach*] Twenty-four hours to the day. Can sleep most of them. Then you've only got the night to work around . . . [*He sighs, puts on glasses, reads.*] "Delores Philipson. Beloved wife of Harris Philipson. Mother of Joyce and Helen Philipson. Funeral services to be held . . ." [*laughs as light dims*]

[*darkness*]

THE
WONDERFULL
YEARE

Preface to
THE WONDERFULL YEARE

The Wonderfull Yeare has to do with the commedia dell'arte. What is therefore necessary for a successful production of the play is a great deal of understanding between the actors of the drama. There is a great deal of room for improvisation and Lazzi. The burden of improvisation falls heaviest on Doña Muerte (the female embodiment of death), Uncle Tío, and the three Women. Doña Muerte should be utilized wherever possible; she is the first to stand at the *Para Distinción* Award dinner, she is also the first to arrive at the funeral of Misserimus' mother. Misserimus makes obscene gestures at her throughout the play. Uncle Tío is much more than a background figure. He, more than Don Hernando, must symbolize the quixotic gentleman. Most of the time on stage he is seen smoking and soaking his feet, always dressed in his beret. The Women may range from old slatterns to active prostitutes who try at various occasions to seduce Misserimus. The play—and the issues it concerns—must have nothing to do with the temporal 1970's, it has to do with always. Another strong figure throughout the play is Gonzalez and his funeral home. He is urbane and politic, he typifies the middle-class Machiavellian merchant who must needs always win in the end.

This play will not be appreciated for some time, but the author has little else to do more worthwhile than waiting.

Edgar White
A.M.D.G.
February, 1970

DRAMATIS PERSONAE

(*In order of appearance*)

FIRST OLD WOMAN
SECOND OLD WOMAN
MISSERIMUS
DON HERNANDO HIDALGO, *Misserimus' father*
MAMACITA, *Misserimus' mother*
UNCLE TÍO, *Misserimus' uncle*
TOMASIO ⎱
MILTON   ⎰ *Misserimus' friends*
RAUL
LOPEZ ⎱
FELIPE   ⎰ *Puerto Rican merchants*
RICARDO
CADIZ
GONZALEZ, *owner of funeral home*
STRANGER
FIRST ATTENDANT
SECOND ATTENDANT
THIRD ATTENDANT
DOÑA MUERTE
MARIA PINEDA
CONSUELA, *Misserimus' sister*
ESTEBAN, *Consuela's husband*
MRS. SANCHEZ
FIRST DETECTIVE
SECOND DETECTIVE
LANDLORD
ROSA MUNDI

SCENE ONE

[*New York slums. Two* OLD WOMEN, *slattern, are throwing dice and prophesying ruin.*]

FIRST OLD WOMAN.   *Los ojos del gato*
                    Las dentes de ratas

SECOND OLD WOMAN.   *La vida es una cloaca*
                     La vida es una cloaca

FIRST OLD WOMAN.   *Hoy is la fetcha de la muerte*
                    Hoy is la fetcha de la muerte

[*They laugh.*]

SECOND OLD WOMAN. *La vida es una cloaca*
La vida es una cloaca

[*They creep offstage, laughing.*]

SCENE TWO

[DON HERNANDO's *apartment. Enter* MISSERIMUS;
*he is dressed in dungarees, a jacket, plaid shirt,
tie and cap. His trousers are bespotted with paint.
He takes wine bottle from pocket and drinks.
Sprinkles salt from his jacket pocket in a circle
around him.* (*A protective symbol.*) *Looks out at
audience and speaks.*]

MISSERIMUS. *Era del año estación florida.* It was the flowery
season of the year. The night has died and it's morning
now. The tenement houses are making love to the skies
and the city is putting on colors. [*takes drink and sighs*]
I am Misserimus Hidalgo, my father's son. They say
I am a painter. The newspaper, *El Diario,* called me
the Puerto Rican Picasso. [*pause*] I don't feel like the
Puerto Rican Picasso, though. I had a brother, Salvador,
but he got killed four years ago. He was always trying
out crazy schemes.

[MAMACITA *enters with a broom and starts to
sweep up salt. She is a plumpish woman, about
forty-five.*]

MISSERIMUS. Ah, Mamacita. [*kisses her on forehead*] My mother
is Puerto Rican, but my father is from Spain, Castilian.
Right, Mama?

MAMACITA. [*smiling shyly*] Yes, from Madrid.

MISSERIMUS. I was speaking about Salvador. One day he and some other guys robbed a liquor store; he was on guard outside. The police came. The gang was running away when Salvador tripped in some dog shit.

MAMACITA. Misserimus!

MISSERIMUS. *Oh, lo siento, Mamacita,* he slipped in some dog excrement, and then got shot in the head by the police. Everyone sent flowers and stuff. Papa's boss sent a whole bunch of pretty flowers. Weren't they pretty, Mamacita?

MAMACITA. Yes, very pretty.

MISSERIMUS. Mama said that Salvador wasn't dead, that he was in heaven. [*pause*] He looked pretty dead to me, though. That was five years ago, wasn't it, Mama?

MAMACITA. [*stops sweeping to muse*] Let me see. Your cousin Rosalita was confirmed three years ago . . . Yes, it must be five years in January.

MISSERIMUS. [*stares out as though looking through window*] Oh, look, the Catholic schoolgirls are going in. How pretty they look. I wonder what they wear beneath their dresses.

[*Enter* DON HERNANDO. *He is in his late forties; wears white suit and suspenders.* MAMACITA *hurries to get his jacket for him.*]

MISSERIMUS. Oh, that's Papa. If you would ask Papa, he would say these are dark times for the Spanish soul. [*turns to Father*] Papacito?

DON HERNANDO. These are indeed dark times for the Spanish soul.

MISSERIMUS. And the Spanish body too, Papa.

DON HERNANDO. [*Staring at bathroom door. He knocks, looks impatiently at watch and at* MAMACITA.] Every morning, every morning. What the hell does he do, live in there?

MAMACITA. [*excitedly*] Uncle! Uncle! Don Hernando must go to work, please, hurry up.

[UNCLE TÍO, *a little old man, dressed in pajamas, a scarf, and a beret, comes stumbling out of bathroom. Stares at them over his shoulder and says nothing. A newspaper is tucked under his arm. He passes.*]

DON HERNANDO. I swear, he must do it just to spite me. Every morning, every morning.

MAMACITA. I am sorry, my husband. My uncle is very old.

[DON HERNANDO *exits to bathroom*]

MISSERIMUS. Uncle Tío doesn't speak much. Papa works as an orderly in a hospital. He says he is gathering material for his autobiography. He was in the Spanish Civil War, but didn't fight because he says it wasn't fun. [*pause*] There was something else I meant to say, oh yes . . . there is a plague in the city.

[DON HERNANDO *comes out of bathroom. He is being fitted into his white suit jacket by* MAMACITA]

DON HERNANDO. We cannot call it a plague. *El Diario* has not called it a plague.

MISSERIMUS. Yes, Papa, if *El Diario* doesn't say it is a plague, we cannot call it a plague.

DON HERNANDO. My Unamuno. [*Extends hand to his left.* MAMACITA *hands him leatherbound issue of Unamuno's* La Sensivo Tragico De La Vida.]

MISSERIMUS. Papa is a philosopher.

DON HERNANDO. Oh Lord, why must I assume such an awkward position before you?

[MAMACITA *kisses him on both cheeks. He puts on coat.*]

MAMACITA. Remember, Consuela and her husband are coming to dinner tonight. Please, do not be late.

DON HERNANDO. That dentist husband of hers is a bore.

MAMACITA. He is your son-in-law, dear.

DON HERNANDO. He is a dentist and a shadow. All right, all right, I will be home. [*looks at* MISSERIMUS] Come here, niño.

[MISSERIMUS *comes.*]

You have been out all night again. You know it is against the law to stay out at night these days.

MISSERIMUS. Many things are against the law these days.

[DON HERNANDO *slaps him.*]

DON HERNANDO. You make your mother worry. Either stay home or move out. What are the four rules of life?

MISSERIMUS.   Oh, Papa . . .

DON HERNANDO.   What are they?

MISSERIMUS.   Always be kind to women. Never withdraw. Always wash between your legs.

DON HERNANDO.   And?

MISSERIMUS.   Always keep your soul free for God.

DON HERNANDO.   *Bueno.* [*He gives* MISSERIMUS *his outstretched hand.* MISSERIMUS *kisses it.* DON HERNANDO *kisses* MISSERIMUS *on forehead and brushes back his hair. He puts his hat on and leaves.*]

SCENE THREE

[MISSERIMUS *and* MAMACITA. *Later in the morning, after* DON HERNANDO *has left.*]

MISSERIMUS.   [*seated on chair with feet up*] Mamacita, I was just thinking.

MAMACITO.   Thinking what, my son?

MISSERIMUS.   Thinking of what a beautiful person I am.

MAMACITA.   Really?

MISSERIMUS.   Yes. I dreamed the other day that I was walking through the streets of Harlem.

MAMACITA.   Yes?

MISSERIMUS. And all these girls were dropping flowers to me from their fire escapes.

MAMACITA. [*laughing*] How romantic, are you sure they were flowers?

MISSERIMUS. Yes, I'm certain they were flowers. I was pushing them aside with a silver cane which I held in my hands.

MAMACITO. You're too romantic, Misserimus.

MISSERIMUS. It's not easy to be romantic in hell.

MAMACITA. Oh, you've been doing all right.

MISSERIMUS. [*quietly*] Yes, I've been doing all right.

MAMACITA. Do you think this thing will go away?

MISSERIMUS. What thing?

MAMACITA. The plague.

MISSERIMUS. I think so. [*pause*] Maybe.

SCENE FOUR

[*Same location as before. There is a painting of bleeding Christ on the wall with a rosary around the rim.* MISSERIMUS *is seated in an armchair with faded seat covers.*]

VOICE. [*offstage*] *Oye pendejo.*

[silence]

Oye pendejo, Misserimus.

[MISSERIMUS *stirs, goes to window.*]

MISSERIMUS. *Que quere bato?*

VOICE. Milton. Tomasio is here, he came this morning. We're coming down with Raul, all right?

MISSERIMUS. Sure, come on down.

[*Darkness. When the lights come on again four men are seated around the living room.* RAUL, *a serious youth with glasses;* TOMASIO, *dressed simply, like an artist;* MILTON, *in a turtleneck.*]

MISSERIMUS. So I said to her, honey, let me eat you for the revolution.

TOMASIO. What did she say?

MISSERIMUS. She didn't say anything. She slapped my face. Then she left.

TOMASIO. Well, you can't win them all.

MISSERIMUS. I've noticed.

MILTON. [*looks at* RAUL *who didn't laugh at joke*] Raul always looks so serious.

TOMASIO. [*jokingly*] Ssh, he has problems.

MILTON. [*touching* RAUL's *shoulder*] *No vole la pena,* Raul.

RAUL. [*jumping up*] Don't touch me.

MISSERIMUS. Hey, what's the matter, man?

RAUL. I just don't like people to touch me, that's all.

[MILTON *looks at* RAUL *and signals to the others that* RAUL *is crazy.*]

MISSERIMUS. Leave Raul alone, Raul is going to save the Puerto Rican by law. Right, Raul?

RAUL. Listen, I'm just trying to get it all together, that's all.

TOMASIO. Ten years from now he'll have a little office in a dark building, with the title *Abogado* on the door.

MILTON. [*laughing*] Paul Perez, *Abogado*.

RAUL. All right, yeah, that's pretty funny. Everybody is just so funny. That's really wonderful. You know, this world [*pause*] is just a big game.

MILTON. Yeah, so you had to go to law school to learn that.

RAUL. I mean, [*gets up and faces someone in audience*] I mean it takes a man about a thousand years to figure it all out. Except a man doesn't have a thousand years. So he's got to do it in a lifetime, right?

MILTON. Yeah.

RAUL. There's so many different circles, so many different kinds of relationships, and they're connected. You try to figure out why you were born poor, or Puerto Rican, or with a particular family, all of that. And while you're disentangling that, more and more people are coming into your life, cripples, young people dying. And you try to get all that shit together. What does it mean?

TOMASIO. Why bother? It never makes sense anyway.

RAUL. Because it has to make some kind of sense. I can't believe all of this happened by accident. It takes a lifetime to make sense out of it. I'm just starting, I don't have it together yet. There are too many faces but someday, it's got to make sense.

MILTON. It's all about politics, man. It's all about going out there and getting it out in the streets. You know?

RAUL. That's just one part, man; that's just one part.

TOMASIO. Fuck politics. Listen, I saw that painting you did of the "Madonna in Chains," Misserimus. I liked it. I really liked it.

MISSERIMUS. Thanks.

MILTON. I liked it, too, except you didn't paint any chains.

TOMASIO. He didn't have to put in any chains, the chains were in her eyes, you get it. Dummy.

[MISSERIMUS *laughs*]

MILTON. Yeah, I know all that symbolism bullshit but I want to see the chains. You called it "Madonna in Chains," let me see the goddamn chains.

TOMASIO. I would have just painted the chains and no Madonna. But it's Misserimus' painting. He's involved with beauty and all of that. I'm more interested in ugliness, but I can still dig his work, you know?

MISSERIMUS. I just paint what amuses me, at the time. That's all.

184 THE WONDERFULL YEARE

TOMASIO. Well, I'm the opposite. I paint what hurts me.

MILTON. But you have to reflect your politics in your work. You can't help it.

MISSERIMUS. Listen, do you remember the painting I did in . . . when was it, December?

TOMASIO. Which one?

MISSERIMUS. The "Señorita."

TOMASIO. Yes.

MISSERIMUS. Well, when I did that one I was working in an empty apartment, on the top floor. There wasn't any steam and I was freezing. So, I was trying to pawn my radio for a heater. I passed this car on the street, a real expensive car, and inside was this really rich girl.

MILTON. That's what you usually find in expensive cars.

TOMASIO. So she gave you the money to buy a heater, right, because she felt sorry for a poor starving artist.

MISSERIMUS. You kidding? Of course not. She just drove away in the back of her heated car.

[*They laugh.*]

But what interested me was the irony of it. I mean she was beautiful and rich. I like rich girls, they smell good, and they taste good, and I like the way silk feels.

RAUL. Everyone should be allowed to be rich.

MISSERIMUS. No, then it wouldn't be any fun to be rich. Anyway, she just looked good. I was glad that somebody in the world was doing all right. You know I don't want everyone to like me. So I painted her from memory.

MILTON. The "Señorita," yeah, I remember now, but I thought you were attacking rich people in that painting.

MISSERIMUS. No, see, I wasn't attacking anyone. I was just painting what I saw.

RAUL. You thing it's funny that someone can be starving in one room and the person right next door doesn't want what he has?

MISSERIMUS. No, what I think is funny is that neither has the slightest idea of the other's existence.

RAUL. That's funny?

TOMASIO. No, no, Raul, he doesn't mean that it's funny that someone is starving. He means . . . oh, what's the fucking use. That's why you're not an artist.

RAUL. Well, I think the world is a very sad place.

TOMASIO. No fooling! Did you hear that, Misserimus? The world's a sad place.

MISSERIMUS. Yeah, I know, I read it in a book the other day. It said the world's a very sad place.

MILTON. [laughing] Did you underline it?

MISSERIMUS. No, I tore it out.

RAUL. It takes a thousand years.

TOMASIO. I spent three months in the country trying to paint.

MISSERIMUS.   You took Alicia with you, didn't you?

TOMASIO.   Yeah, you ever been locked up for three months with an idiot?

MISSERIMUS.   Alicia?

TOMASIO.   Yeah, Alicia, what a pain in the ass. "Tomasio, what are you doing?" I'm thinking. "What are you thinking?" I'm thinking about strangling you bitch.

[*They laugh.*]

It snowed every day. I didn't get anything done. And what's worse, I think she's pregnant.

MISSERIMUS.   Good Catholic, Puerto Rican girl, I'm sure she loves being pregnant.

TOMASIO.   You know, man, I'm twenty-eight years old. I'm getting hemorrhoids from sitting, my eyes are going bad from painting, I'm a nervous wreck. For what? For art, so they can say you're derivative. I'm derivative of my goddamn mother and father.

MISSERIMUS.   Illegitimately.

RAUL.   The Puerto Rican . . .

TOMASIO.   [*calmly*] Raul, shut up.

RAUL.   All right.

TOMASIO.   As for the Puerto Rican, have you ever tried to give a grocer or a butcher a painting in exchange for food, or rent?

MISSERIMUS.   [*laughing*] Oh yeah.

TOMASIO.   Right, forget it.

RAUL.   Our people aren't educated toward art yet.

TOMASIO.   Well, what the fuck should I do while they're learning, starve?

MISSERIMUS.   Listen, you're going to lose anyway so . . .

TOMASIO.   So?

MISSERIMUS.   So you have your choice of how you want to lose. Once you know that you're going to fail anyway, you're perfectly free.

RAUL.   Free?

MILTON.   He means relatively, Raul.

TOMASIO.   Is that supposed to make me happy?

MISSERIMUS.   It's the best I can do for you today. Ask me again tomorrow, I'll have another answer for you.

MILTON.   Hey, listen, there's a meeting of the Puerto Rican merchants at the Gonzalez Funeral Home.

TOMASIO.   At the funeral home?

MILTON.   Yeah, who knows why. So anyway, you want to go?

TOMASIO.   No, I have to go to the doctor.

MISSERIMUS.   I'll go.

MILTON.   Raul?

RAUL. I have to go study.

TOMASIO. Of course. You know, [*pause*] it's a drag to be bourgeois when you don't even have the money to be bourgeois.

RAUL. What do you mean by that?

TOMASIO. Nothing.

SCENE FIVE

[*The Gonzalez Funeral Home. About twelve middle-aged men are sitting around. The owner of a grocery store speaks to* FELIPE. *A casket is visible, bearing the signs:* REQUIESCAT IN PACE *and* EXPECTATIONS RESURRECTIONEM MORTUORIUM.]

LOPEZ. Well, Felipe, this is the best you could do for a meeting place?

FELIPE. It's not my fault, something went wrong with the electricity in the Civic Building.

LOPEZ. But a funeral home, Felipe?

FELIPE. [*shrugging*] Pues.

LOPEZ. This is the last time that you are in charge of facilities. And look at the refreshment! Beer. Cadiz owns a liquor store, the least he could have brought was some Bacardi or some wine or something.

CADIZ. What is that you are saying about me behind my back, Lopez? Do you think me a millionaire?

GONZALEZ. [*laughing*] Come, come, my friends, no need to argue. Welcome to my humble establishment, you will all be visiting here someday.

[*very little laughter in response*]

Oh, come on now, we might as well have a bit of humor.

LOPEZ. You are too happy being a funeral director, Gonzalez.

GONZALEZ. I enjoy my work. I'm very busy these days.

LOPEZ. I bet you are.

[*enter* MISSERIMUS *and* MILTON]

Well, what have we here?

MILTON. We represent the Puerto Rican artist.

LOPEZ. What Puerto Rican artist? We have none.

MISSERIMUS. That's why we must represent them. You still have a very nice funeral parlor, Gonzalez, I remember my brother was here.

GONZALEZ. Oh yes, they had all those pretty flowers, that's right.

MISSERIMUS. Yes.

GONZALEZ. I remember your father read something very beautiful.

MISSERIMUS. Yes. Gongora.

GONZALEZ. How is Don Hidalgo?

MISSERIMUS. Quite well, thank you.

LOPEZ. Well, we might as well begin. Ricardo, do you want to begin the meeting, please.

RICARDO. [*A pimply faced* nouveau riche. *He wears glasses, and attempts to affect power. Clears his throat and begins speaking.*] Yes, this meeting of the Puerto Rican Merchants Guild will now convene.

MILTON. [*to* MISSERIMUS] Will now convene, that's good. Pass me a beer, please, Misserimus.

[MISSERIMUS *passes the beer.*]

RICARDO. Fellow merchants, the purpose of this gathering is to decide what course of action would be most . . . um . . . advantageous for us to pursue in establishing ourselves as reputable businessmen. The day of the lonely *bodega* owner is long past. I think that we should incorporate ourselves, and hire a lawyer to draw up a contract. Our only hope of gaining power is to make ourselves a persuasive unit in the American business world.

LOPEZ. That sounds sensible to me.

CADIZ. *Sin duda, sin duda.*

RICARDO. Gentlemen, we know that now our position is a small and powerless one. However, as the Irish, the Italian, and the Jew, we can become an active member of the American business world.

CADIZ. Should we try to associate with the Negro Business Guild?

RICARDO. I think not, at least not now. We need our separate identity. We must make the name of the Puerto Rican a prominent one in its own right.

MILTON.   Señors, only the Negro has befriended us. He has shown us how to survive in the worst city in the world. If we do not ally ourselves with him now . . .

RICARDO.   The Negro has taught us how to steal, take dope, and run numbers; that has been his gift to us.

MILTON.   These, too, were necessary to learn.

RICARDO.   We would have done far better without it. We have to change our image or else we shall never move from the station in which . . .

[enter young Puerto Rican, obviously on drugs]

STRANGER.   Hey . . . hey man . . . I . . .

CADIZ.   Who are you?

GONZALEZ.   What do you want here?

STRANGER.   Wow man . . . I just want to cop some sleep, you know . . . Just let me squat here for a minute.

GONZALEZ.   Let you what? Is this a friend of yours?

MILTON.   Every brother is my friend.

STRANGER.   Yeah, brother . . . talk on, baby . . . tell them I just want to fall out here for a minute.

GONZALEZ.   This is a funeral home.

STRANGER.   A funeral home, wow . . . That's O.K., man, I don't want to stay forever, just for a minute, you know.

GONZALEZ.   I'm sorry, but you can't.

[*Several usher him out.*]

STRANGER.   Oh man, what a drag. I just want to come down, you know.

GONZALEZ.   Out!

STRANGER.   [*at door*] Hey man, can I come back if I die?

GONZALEZ.   Yes, if you die you can come back here, take one of my cards. Do you have parents?

STRANGER.   Parents? . . . I don't remember, man.

GONZALEZ.   They're probably trying to forget, too.

[STRANGER *leaves.*]

RICARDO.   All right, let's take a vote. All those in favor of a Puerto Rican association without Negroes, say aye.

[*All say aye.*]

The ayes have it. Next on the agenda.

MILTON.   You have sold yourselves to the *blancos,* the white race still has you. You are all *gusanos,* and after the revolution . . .

ALL.   Revolution. The revolution. Get out of here, fool. Puerto Rican artist, eh.

MILTON.   Here we are, here are our people locked in a funeral home. You'll never leave the tenements.

MISSERIMUS. Ten thousand years from the cave to the tenement building. Mankind is making progress, Milton.

GONZALEZ. Please, leave.

MILTON. All right, I'll call you if I die.

GONZALEZ. Don't bother. You don't have the money.

MISSERIMUS. [*taking several cans of beer, takes one from the hands of* LOPEZ] Thank you all, have a good business guild.

[MILTON *and* MISSERIMUS *move toward the door, away from others.*]

MISSERIMUS. Well, I'm going to see Maria Pineda.

MILTON. You don't see Anna anymore?

MISSERIMUS. No.

MILTON. Remember when she chased you to Lenox Avenue with a switchblade?

MISSERIMUS. Anna is a very spirited girl.

MILTON. Yes, well, I always say, every woman has her way of fucking.

MISSERIMUS. Is that what you always say?

MILTON. Whenever I'm asked.

MISSERIMUS. I don't remember asking.

MILTON. Well anyway. [*makes the sign of cross*] Requiescat in pace.

SCENE SIX

[*The hospital where* DON HERNANDO *works. Simple setting.* DON HERNANDO *is dressed in a blue custodian's uniform. He is leaning on a broom, pausing for a moment to plan methodically how to go about sweeping the floor. As the scene progresses, several of his friends, dressed in similar outfits, circle around him. The parts of the* ATTENDANTS *should be played by the same actors who were in the funeral parlor, in the previous scene.*]

DON HERNANDO. My, I wonder what would be the best way to go about this. Yesterday I swept the dirt straight on until I reached the steps. Then I swept everything down the steps. That took me twenty minutes. The day before that I swept the steps first and then did the hall. That took me eighteen minutes. But I was very energetic that day, whereas I was very tired yesterday. So I guess it's the same difference. Maybe if

[*pause*]

I swept everything to this side and then went over everything once more to make certain. Then I would probably save five minutes. This way is more artistic though. So many people come into the hospital these days, that it doesn't really make a difference how you clean.

[*pause*]

God, I didn't think that little girl was going to die, though. Such a little thing . . .

[*Other* ATTENDANTS *come on stage, laughing and carrying on a conversation.*]

FIRST ATTENDANT. No, I'm not lying, man.

SECOND ATTENDANT. Oh, come on now.

FIRST ATTENDANT. No, really. Maria, the dietician, has a thing for me.

THIRD ATTENDANT. Why you?

FIRST ATTENDANT. I don't know. Because I'm so pretty, I guess.

[*They laugh.*]

SECOND ATTENDANT. She's a young girl though.

FIRST ATTENDANT. She's not so young.

THIRD ATTENDANT. How old you think, about sixteen?

FIRST ATTENDANT. No, about twenty.

SECOND ATTENDANT. Oh, come on! She's just beginning to have breasts.

FIRST ATTENDANT. No, they're small, that's all.

THIRD ATTENDANT. Don Hernando.

DON HERNANDO. Yes, I hear you.

THIRD ATTENDANT. What do you think?

DON HERNANDO. I don't have time to be involved in your foolish conversations.

THIRD ATTENDANT. Oh, you have more important things to think on, eh?

DON HERNANDO. Yes.

SECOND ATTENDANT. Like sweeping floors.

[*They laugh.*]

DON HERNANDO. [*dryly*] We all sweep floors, Felipe.

FIRST ATTENDANT. But not like you do, Don Hernando.

THIRD ATTENDANT. Yes, he does it with such grace.

[THIRD ATTENDANT *mimics* DON HERNANDO's *movements with broom. The others laugh, then grow silent as* DON HERNANDO *continues to sweep.*]

FIRST ATTENDANT. Heh, Don Hernando, give us a *cante hondo*.

SECOND ATTENDANT. Yes, *cante hondo*, Don Hernando, *conte hondo*.

DON HERNANDO. I have no time now.

SECOND ATTENDANT. Oh, come on.

[DON HERNANDO *pauses. Thinks for a second and then goes up to the others leaning on his broom.*]

DON HERNANDO. O.K.

[*There is a long pause and then he begins.*]

There is nothing comparable to my song.

FIRST ATTENDANT.   Yes! Yes! *Eso es cante hondo.*

DON HERNANDO.   I'll tell you of my sadness.

FIRST ATTENDANT.   Your sadness, Don Hernando?

DON HERNANDO.   Yes. That. I was thinking of Death a while ago. It was very strange because I first became aware of Her, Death, when I was sixteen years old.

SECOND ATTENDANT.   Yes, sing! Sing!

DON HERNANDO.   I was out very late drinking with my college friends. We were young, we didn't care. I could drink more than all of them and still speak clearly of Aristotle.

THIRD ATTENDANT.   Who?

DON HERNANDO.   Never mind. Anyway, one evening I was walking home. I felt so easy and free listening to the sounds of my footsteps. The gates of the city had already closed. I was alone, the little stars behind me and my two shadows going before.

I come along a broken stream and the fish were laughing. The trees bent over me and I thought they were in love with me. I saw three hanging branches and they looked like little moorish girls. I mean they made me think of three moorish girls.

SECOND ATTENDANT.   Life is a drunken man.

DON HERNANDO. Yes, life is a drunken man. I thought it was pretty there so I sat down by a rock.

FIRST ATTENDANT. Only reasonable.

DON HERNANDO. Then, I thought I heard birds singing but I knew it was too early for the birds to be singing. It seemed very strange to me. The birds sang and it was a stronger singing than I had ever heard before. I suddenly felt a cold chill then, I felt that I was dying.

SECOND ATTENDANT. [*in joy*] *Que bueno.*

THIRD ATTENDANT. Yes, *que bueno.*

DON HERNANDO. I knew then that everything in the world was dying. Birds, trees, the grass, the water, everything.

FIRST ATTENDANT. Best not to think on it too much.

DON HERNANDO. I thought about the girl whom I had first made love to. A Venezuelan girl. Very nice family.

FIRST ATTENDANT. I knew a Venezuelan girl, that good, but a lot of trouble. She had great big . . .

DON HERNANDO. This is my *cante hondo.*

FIRST ATTENDANT. Oh yes, sorry.

DON HERNANDO. I felt as if I was leaping into space. Someplace between two mountains, and I moved my legs because I thought I was flying so gracefully. I felt myself touching the ground softly, very softly. You know the way you fall after you've just made love.

FIRST ATTENDANT. Eh, yes! yes! *Chico, es verdad.*

DON HERNANDO. Yes, that softly. And then as I touched the ground the birds stopped their singing.

FIRST ATTENDANT. [*speaking to* SECOND ATTENDANT] He's from Spain you know.

SECOND ATTENDANT. Yes, I know.

DON HERNANDO. When I first met my wife, I didn't think a man could love a woman so much and still be sane. She had the blackest eyes. [*pause*] My son, Misserimus, has her eyes. [*pause*] He's a good son and talented, very talented.

FIRST ATTENDANT. He paints, doesn't he?

THIRD ATTENDANT. Yes, *El Diario* called him the Puerto Rican Picasso.

FIRST ATTENDANT. [*in amazement*] Oh, ah hah!

DON HERNANDO. Her hair was thick then, and I used to say it was like the branches in Sevilla. Her grandmother used to put olive oil on it, she said it made it shine. And she used to wear a kerchief around it. I brought the kerchief from my house, it was my mother's, a large silk one with red embroidery around the edges. I first met her in Puerto Rico, it was very different then. The United States didn't own it. It didn't say black or white on your birth certificate then. I don't remember when I first decided to marry her. It all happened very quickly. The next thing I knew I was waiting for my first child to be born. I came into the room and the place smelled of birth. A damp, thick smell, a little like blood except different, you know?

FIRST ATTENDANT. Oh yes! I know.

DON HERNANDO. Then they put this little thing into my arms. It was so tiny, I didn't think anything could be so tiny and live. Yet, it made such a big lump inside her.

[*They laugh.*]

That was Salvador, my first. He was always strange until . . . [*sighs*] There have been times that I felt happy.

FIRST ATTENDANT. Happy?

DON HERNANDO. Yes, happy, so happy, that I thought God would get jealous.

SECOND ATTENDANT. *Olé!* Don Hernando, *olé!*

DON HERNANDO. Yes, times when I was happy and wasn't afraid of the world. I was a man at his table with others looking on with respect. But now it's *nothing* that I feel.

FIRST ATTENDANT. Nothing?

DON HERNANDO. Yes nothing, a space between happy and sad, the place which all the days and all the years, and all the streets and all the hospitals fill up.

SECOND ATTENDANT. [*drawing close to* DON HERNANDO] Is it death that you mean?

DON HERNANDO. No, it's the thing other than life that I mean.

SECOND ATTENDANT. It is a time of loose wind.

SCENE SEVEN

[*The home of* MARIA PINEDA *and her aunt,* DOÑA
MUERTA. *On the wall are the portraits of Martin
Luther King and the two Kennedys.* MARIA *is
seated on a couch, doing her fingernails. She
has her hair tied behind.* DOÑA MUERTE *is dressed
in black. She is in her late forties.*]

DOÑA.   Why do you have to do your nails in the living room?

MARIA.   Oh, *Tía.*

[*There is a knock.*]

DOÑA.   I'll get it. [*goes to door*] Oh, it's you.

MISSERIMUS.   [*seizing* DOÑA MUERTE *in his arms*] Oh Doña, I am
mad for you.

DOÑA.   Get away from me, you nut. Maria, it's that crazy Misserimus.

MARIA.   [*jumping up, then collecting herself*] Oh!

[MARIA *freezes, perfectly still. Enter* MISSERI-
MUS. *He is carrying flowers.*]

MISSERIMUS.   This is Doña Muerte. She is the aunt of Maria
Pineda. She raised Maria from an infant when her
parents gave her up. She is a sad woman and hates all

men, particularly Puerto Rican men. Her eyes are filled with dying. Her hands are too thin.

[MISSERIMUS *walks about* DOÑA. DOÑA *takes the flowers which* MISSERIMUS *has brought.*]

DOÑA. He probably stole them.

MARIA. Doña Muerte, don't say that.

DOÑA. Well, I suppose I should put these in water.

MISSERIMUS. She is so sad. [*kisses* DOÑA *softly, takes a flower from her and sits down on couch*]

MISSERIMUS. This is Maria Pineda. Her thighs are like an Ingres. Her breasts are small, dancer's breasts; they are a Degas. [*gets up and slowly walks about her*] Her stomach has a nice roundness here. Good to roll on and make love. Her eyes are the sad eyes of a Soutine. [*kisses her softly on the mouth*] She has good strong legs from dancing. [*sits down*]

MARIA. Well, I haven't seen you in five months. Nice of you to just drop in. How is Anna?

MISSERIMUS. I don't know.

MARIA. Oh.

MISSERIMUS. Yes. Oh.

[*exit* DOÑA MUERTE]

MARIA. How are you?

MISSERIMUS. I'm as I was. And you?

MARIA.   I have a cold.

MISSERIMUS.   [*staring at her black sailor's trousers*] My, my, there's a lot of buttons on those pants, it must take a long time to get them loose.

MARIA.   Never mind my buttons.

MISSERIMUS.   All right. [*pause*] I like the little V that your thighs make.

MARIA.   Is that all you think about?

MISSERIMUS.   [*pause*] Yes.

MARIA.   Well, don't come to me for that.

MISSERIMUS.   Maria Pineda, I am quite taken with you.

MARIA.   Oh.

MISSERIMUS.   You should be on a great stallion, with your hair down. Riding softly along the shadowy mountains.

MARIA.   Oh, here we go again.

[*enter* DOÑA MUERTE]

DOÑA.   Well, I guess I'll just put these on top of here. It would have been more practical to get artificial ones, they last longer.

MISSERIMUS.   But they're not as beautiful, Doña Muerte.

DOÑA.   Not as beautiful. Ha, what's beauty?

MISSERIMUS.   Maria is beauty.

DOÑA.   You can't eat beauty.

MISSERIMUS. [*looking at* MARIA] I'd like to try.

DOÑA. What?

MISSERIMUS. Nothing.

DOÑA. How is your crazy father?

MISSERIMUS. All right. Thank you.

DOÑA. You drop out of college, eh?

MISSERIMUS. Yes.

DOÑA. Why, you're not suppose to be stupid?

MISSERIMUS. They had no more to teach, I had no more to learn.

DOÑA. Now, what will you do, paint?

MISSERIMUS. Yes.

DOÑA. Do you know what the rule of life is?

MISSERIMUS. Always wash between your legs?

DOÑA. What?

MISSERIMUS. Nothing.

DOÑA. The rule is, always have backing.

MISSERIMUS. Oh. That's a very good rule.

DOÑA. You'll find out just how good it is when you're starving in some ghetto.

MISSERIMUS. You'll always feed me, won't you, Doña Muerte?

DOÑA. Me? Ha! Don't count on me. Well, I have to get to work. I have no parents supporting me. [*puts on black coat*]

MARIA. *Tía!*

MISSERIMUS. You know, I think you're trying to be offensive, Doña Muerte.

DOÑA. [*disregarding him*] Well, good-bye. [*kisses* MARIA]

MARIA. Good-bye, *Tía.*

[*exit* DOÑA MUERTE]

MISSERIMUS. Well, Maria Pineda, my little Puerto Rican lady.

[MARIA *sits beside him*]

MARIA. I'm not your little Puerto Rican lady, I'm not Puerto Rican, dammit.

MISSERIMUS. Of course, you're Puerto Rican. Your ass is too large to be a white girl's, your eyes are too dark, your hair is too beautiful, you can't be white.

MARIA. So for you I've got to wear red lace panties, and live in badly decorated houses, eat rice and beans, and stink of garlic.

MISSERIMUS. You have a nice strong body, good for going out and supporting your man; nice breasts for giving milk to babies, it will make them rounder.

MARIA. Yes, I have to drop babies like a cow for you, eh? So that I can be a good Puerto Rican idiot woman.

MISSERIMUS. You can't deny your people.

MARIA. My parents denied me.

MISSERIMUS. Your parents were unfortunate.

MARIA. And my uncle Carlos did the same thing to Doña Muerte.

MISSERIMUS. Your uncle Carlos was unfortunate.

MARIA. Yes, for you everyone is just unfortunate.

MISSERIMUS. Yes.

MARIA. And what do you want from life?

MISSERIMUS. I want to die and go to the working class section of heaven.

MARIA. Very funny. Never serious, are you?

MISSERIMUS. Not if I can help it.

MARIA. Everything is so strange these days. I'm afraid to go out in the streets. I don't understand what's going on but no one else seems to either.

MISSERIMUS. Yes, I've noticed everyone seems frightened.

MARIA. And so many police, all over.

MISSERIMUS. Yes, the police are very busy.

MARIA. Is it an epidemic? What's going to happen to me?

MISSERIMUS. To you, nothing. You're going to continue, slipping into flower-print panties; you're going to marry a nice guy with a nice paunch; you're going to have two children two years apart, and you're going to do a happily-ever-after.

MARIA.   You're making fun of me again. What's wrong with wanting a decent home? What's wrong with wanting some security? Why do people have to live like animals? I want to get out of this city before I get old. Everybody is so tired, so sick. I just want some peace.

MISSERIMUS.   A little garden?

MARIA.   All right, a little garden.

MISSERIMUS.   Don't get angry, I like little gardens.

MARIA.   Doña Muerte is right, you need backing to do anything in this world.

MISSERIMUS.   Doña Muerte is always right.

MARIA.   You don't like her, do you?

MISSERIMUS.   She's all right.

MARIA.   I have great respect for her. She raised me and my brother all by herself.

MISSERIMUS.   She sent you to ballet school, taught you how to play the piano, that's important.

MARIA.   You think it's funny, I enjoyed it.

MISSERIMUS.   You're a nice little Puerto Rican girl. What's your brother doing?

MARIA.   He has a good job with the post office, he lives in

Queens, now. His wife is having a baby. He's getting a promotion soon.

MISSERIMUS. To what?

MARIA. I don't know, in charge of the dead letter office, I think.

MISSERIMUS. Oh, gosh! I wanted to be the first Puerto Rican in charge of the dead letter office.

MARIA. [angry] At least he's working. He isn't trying to rob liquor stores.

MISSERIMUS. Tsh. Tsh. You want to hurt me. That's not nice.

MARIA. It's not nice to make fun of my brother either. Oh, why do I fight with you all the time?

MISSERIMUS. Because I remind you who you are.

MARIA. I know who I am.

MISSERIMUS. No, you don't.

MARIA. Is there anything wrong in having some pride in yourself, in wanting to advance?

MISSERIMUS. No, nothing's wrong with that, but if you try and forget your people, your background, a lot is wrong.

MARIA. The Puerto Ricans have nothing to offer me.

MISSERIMUS. They have everything to offer you.

MARIA. Like what, syphillis, welfare, and bad teeth?

MISSERIMUS. No, just your identity.

MARIA. You can't eat identity.

MISSERIMUS. Come here, honey.

MARIA. [*gets up*] What do you want?

MISSERIMUS. I'm going to tell you the story of the Spanish Civil War.

MARIA. You mean the one in Spain?

MISSERIMUS. Yes. [*takes her hands*] You see, all the country was one body, just like yours. Your breasts are Sevilla and Barcelona. Your thighs, this one is the worker and this one is the fascist. And the little thing you have here in the middle . . . [*she slaps his hand as he goes to touch it.*] This is the center, what they believe to be the Spanish tradition, and do you know how stupid it all was, because it's all just one body.

MARIA. Your father was there then, wasn't he?

MISSERIMUS. Yes. But he didn't fight.

MARIA. Why?

MISSERIMUS. Because he said it wasn't fun.

MARIA. Oh. You have pretty eyes, Misserimus.

MISSERIMUS. So do you.

MARIA. No I don't, I don't like my eyes. They're the wrong eyes.

MISSERIMUS. Oh.

MARIA. Why did you really quit school?

MISSERIMUS. They wanted to save me. Save the Puerto Rican kid, ladies and gentlemen. I learned to paint at the youth center. I got in college, majored in fine arts, whatever the hell that is. They messed me up so much, I couldn't see colors anymore. My eyes were dead. My soul was dead. So I split.

MARIA. You should have finished.

MISSERIMUS. No, honey. The only thing I'm supposed to do is keep my soul, and keep moving until they get me.

MARIA. Until who gets you?

MISSERIMUS. The people in power.

MARIA. Why do they want to get you?

MISSERIMUS. Because I'm too happy.

MARIA. You're not so happy.

MISSERIMUS. Then because I'm too bad.

MARIA. Oh.

MISSERIMUS. There's a grave waiting for me.

MARIA. A grave.

MISSERIMUS. Yes, it was made before I was born. It's just a matter of time. It was all charted out a long time ago.

MARIA. You make me scared.

MISSERIMUS. Don't be. Come. We've done enough talking. There's nothing more to say. It's time.

MARIA.   [*startled*] Time for what?

MISSERIMUS.   Time to get into some very serious loving.

MARIA.   What?

[*He starts to unbutton her pants.*]

You can't just undress me.

MISSERIMUS.   You're right, I can't.

MARIA.   I don't even know you, really.

MISSERIMUS.   You know me, I'm a happy Puerto Rican kid.

MARIA.   Is that what you are?

MISSERIMUS.   Hmmm, can't get these damn buttons loose. Hold
on, I've got a knife. [*takes out switchblade*]

MARIA.   It's all right, I'll take them off. We'll have to hurry.
She'll be home soon.

MISSERIMUS.   We have lots of time. [*looks at her standing in
underwear*] My, my, my, *concha Madra de Dios.* [*gets
on his knees and rubs head on her belly*] This isn't a
bad way to spend the time while waiting for the revolution.

SCENE EIGHT

[*The home of* MISSERIMUS. *The table is elabo-rately set for the dinner.* DON HERNANDO *enters. He looks weary and confused. He stands in the doorway taking off his coat.* MAMACITA *comes out.*]

MAMACITA.   Ah, you're home. Good, they'll be here soon. What's the matter? [*kisses him*]

DON HERNANDO.   I've lost my Unamuno.

MAMACITA.   No!

DON HERNANDO.   Yes, I don't know, I must be getting old. I remember I had it before I went on the train. I bought the evening paper . . . and then I noticed it was gone.

MAMACITA.   Don't worry. You'll get another.

DON HERNANDO.   But that one was autographed.

MAMACITA.   And such a beautiful leather cover, too.

DON HERNANDO.   Every day I forget one more thing. A man's head empties daily. By the time I die I will be a complete idiot.

MAMACITA.   Oh, come now. Get yourself together. They will be here soon.

DON HERNANDO. I can't stand company tonight.

MAMACITA. Well . . .

[*the sound of knocking*]

They're here. [*goes to door*]

[*Enter the daughter* CONSUELA *and* ESTEBAN. *He is youngish, in his thirties, very stocky with a crew haircut.*]

MAMACITA. Ah, Consuela. [*Kisses her and* ESTEBAN. *Takes their coats.* CONSUELA *leaves on her silk scarf, ties it tightly about her neck. She is tastefully dressed. He is dressed in a dark suit.*] Oh, you smell so good.

CONSUELA. It's a new perfume. Do you like it, Mamacita? Oh, Papa. [*kisses him*]

DON HERNANDO. You're looking well, Consuela. Esteban, how are you? [*shakes his hand*]

ESTEBAN. Quite well, thank you.

CONSUELA. Where is Misserimus and Uncle Tío?

MAMACITA. Uncle Tío is sleeping as usual. I don't know where Misserimus is. Consuela, come and help me with the food, let the men speak.

[*They exit.*]

ESTEBAN. Well, Don Hernando, are you still writing?

DON HERNANDO. Yes. I'm still writing. How are things in the teeth business?

ESTEBAN. You mean dentistry.

DON HERNANDO. Yes, I guess that's what I mean.

ESTEBAN. Quite well, you know, can't complain. This epidemic is bad for business.

DON HERNANDO. Oh?

ESTEBAN. Yes, few people are worried about their teeth these days.

[enter CONSUELA, *carrying wine bottle*]

CONSUELA. Can you open this, dear?

ESTEBAN. I'll certainly try.

DON HERNANDO. Come here, Consuela.

[*She comes.*]

Your belly still looks flat. Nothing yet?

CONSUELA. Papacito!

ESTEBAN. We're not quite ready for kids yet.

DON HERNANDO. Not quite ready, you've been married three years. What have you been doing all that time? There's more to life than teeth. I'm getting to be an old man, I want to see my grandchildren before I die.

CONSUELA. You'll have them, Papa. We're just waiting until we're economically more stable.

DON HERNANDO. You young people have a schedule for everything nowadays. You even choose what day they'll be born on. There's no happiness anywhere. Just charts and timetables.

[*enter* MISSERIMUS]

CONSUELA. Ah, Misserimus. [*embraces him*]

ESTEBAN. [*uncorks wine and gives it to* CONSUELA] Well, if it isn't the Puerto Rican Picasso.

MISSERIMUS. How are you, Esteban?

ESTEBAN. We can't stay late, you know. We can't walk the streets late these days. You know, I saw an excellent production of Macbeth in Spanish the other day.

DON HERNANDO. Oh.

ESTEBAN. Yes, they should have more of that. We had great theater in Santo Domingo before the peasants took over.

DON HERNANDO. The peasants.

ESTEBAN. There is nothing now, since Trujillo fell.

CONSUELA. [*sensing an argument*] Yes, it was an excellent production.

ESTEBAN. Yes. [*puts out arm theatrically*] "Mañana, y mañana y mañana que significo mañana?"

CONSUELA. Oh Esteban, that's enough. He thinks he's on stage.

ESTEBAN. Yes, I get carried away. That Shakespeare, oh, there was a writer.

DON HERNANDO. What about Calderón?

MISSERIMUS. And Tirso de Molina?

DON HERNANDO. And Lope de Vega?

ESTEBAN. All right, all right, I'm not disregarding them, but Shakespeare was so . . . so . . .

MISSERIMUS. So quotable.

ESTEBAN. Yes! Anyway, it's good to see that Spanish is becoming a part of the American culture.

DON HERNANDO. American and culture is a contradiction in terms.

MISSERIMUS. That's very good, Papa. A contradiction in terms.

ESTEBAN. Just because I say something about art he argues with me. You don't think I know anything about art, eh? In my way I, too, am an artist.

DON HERNANDO. Making false teeth?

ESTEBAN. I am a prosthetist, a dental prosthetist, and that too is an art.

CONSUELA. All right, Esteban.

ESTEBAN. No. He is always belittling me. Just because I don't live in a fantasy world as he does, writing at night with a quill, cleaning hospital floors all day.

DON HERNANDO. I have no use for a fascist who makes false teeth.

ESTEBAN. Yes, but you didn't mind asking this fascist to lend you money to pay your son's funeral.

CONSUELA. Esteban!

DON HERNANDO. A gentleman would not speak of it.

ESTEBAN. A gentleman would not ask for money.

MAMACITA. [*entering, sees something running across floor*] Aahhh! A rat!

CONSUELA. [*clutching* ESTEBAN] Yes, I saw it.

MISSERIMUS. It was probably just a mouse.

CONSUELA. No. I saw it too, it was large, like a cat.

ESTEBAN. Well, that settles it, I won't have my wife in a place filled with rats.

DON HERNANDO. Get out of my house and never come again. Consuela, if you come you come alone.

ESTEBAN. Come, Consuela; and I want my money back

DON HERNANDO. You will have your money by the end of this month or I will kill myself.

ESTEBAN. I hope so. Come, Consuela.

CONSUELA. Papa . . . I'm sorry . . . [*puts on coat*]

DON HERNANDO. It's all right.

MAMACITA. Wait, I'll leave with you. I'm going to make novena at St. Anthony's. I'll light one for you too, my husband.

DON HERNANDO. Go on, woman.

[*They exit.*]

SCENE NINE

[MAMACITA *is standing before a large candle. The rest of the stage is in darkness.*]

MAMACITA. *Madre de Dios.* [*kneels*] Tonight it is so silent outside. I think all of the children in the world must be sleeping now. Salvador is sleeping. [*pause*] Yes, he must be. Something like snow. Oh Virgin, your eyes are so bright tonight. Maybe it's the candles. [*lights another candle*] Virgin, [*pause, then says in whispering voice*] I wish Don Hernando and the family didn't fight tonight. It doesn't make any sense to fight. Men die so easily. Señora Garcia is usually here at this time. [*looks around her*] I hope nothing has happened to her. So many rats in the city. People pass away so. Sometimes you're speaking to someone and then suddenly they're gone and all you have is voices then. Just like being left in a room filled with voices. Sometimes you remember who the voices are but mostly you forget. Ah, but Consuela smelled so beautiful tonight. I wonder if her husband bought that for her? No, no, a man couldn't feel that much! She must have got it herself. When I see my daughter, Virgin, it's like seeing myself really. That's not so strange, I guess. [*pause*] When she was small she would wear my clothes, and it used to frighten me. The blue one, or was it [*pause*] the green, yes, because my cousin gave me that one.

Mother of God, I didn't sin this week, [*pause*] not that I remember. Oh yes, in the *bodega,* when I was buying the fruit, and he gave me back too much change. But that wasn't . . . well, it was only ten cents. He's cheated many people before. So anyway it was all right.

What could have happened to Señora Garcia? [*looks around again*] Maybe, it was her son Salvador . . . I mean Miguel, Salvador is my . . . well, you know Salvador.

Madonna, I wonder if the night is this quiet everywhere. [*pause*] It's so still you can hear leaves falling. Your colors are blue and white, Madonna. Oh, look, there's a stain there. It looks green in this light. It must have been from the candles. Did I stop that leaking faucet? I went into the kitchen to get my purse. Yes, I must have shut it off. [*pause*] Don Hernando soft and floating. Snoring like that. And he didn't believe that he snored when I told him. But then he laughed. I wonder why I . . . It must have been because that first time he was standing over me like that . . . and I made the joke about the leaking faucet. [*laughs*] Or did he make the joke? Anyway, he was funny. [*Pause. Suddenly grows serious.*] Let me make my prayer, Madonna. Don Hernando says I should be more serious. He's right, it doesn't do for a woman to be silly all the time. They're just like that. Just like a baby at your nipples until they get what they want and then . . . like a sack of wheat. What is it that all men sing for? What is it?

Mother of God, please, keep everyone safe in their houses. Bring them home at the end of the day. Guide them home past death and the crooked streets . . . Home to their . . . home to those that [*pause*] those that want them. Mother of God, keep us unafraid, and bring our house together again. [*makes the sign of the cross and rises to go then suddenly remembers something, turns back*] This rosary, Virgin, was my mother's. [*holds up a silver rosary*] I'll leave it here at your feet, some poor woman will be very grateful, then you will grant me my wish. It's real silver. [*looks at rosary and pauses*] I think, anyway. Good-bye, Virgin.

[*exit*]

SCENE TEN

[DON HERNANDO *and* MISSERIMUS *are seated opposite each other.* DON HERNANDO *smokes a pipe. He gets up and looks out at audience as though looking out of a window.*]

DON HERNANDO. Look how sad the streets look. The houses seem like they are standing for death.

MISSERIMUS. [*stands and looks out also*] The moon looks like a matador.

DON HERNANDO. I lost my Unamuno today.

MISSERIMUS. I'm sorry, Papacito. Shall I read you some Lorca or Cervantes.

DON HERNANDO. Yes, I'm in the mood for some Lorca, I think.

[MISSERIMUS *goes to bookshelf.*]

Why did Consuela have to marry a pig?

MISSERIMUS. Maybe, because she loved him, Papa.

DON HERNANDO. I think he's impotent, too. They should have a child by now.

[*enter* MAMACITA *excitedly*]

MAMACITA. Hernando, Misserimus. You wouldn't believe what just happened.

DON HERNANDO. What now?

MAMACITA. They just arrested Raul.

MISSERIMUS. Raul?

MAMACITA. He must have gone crazy. He was running through the streets naked. He tried to nail up a sign on the church door.

MISSERIMUS. Sign? What did it say?

MAMACITA. I don't know. They pulled it off and carried him away. The streets are filled with police.

MISSERIMUS. Too bad, Raul was a nice guy. He was never very lucky, though.

DON HERNANDO. Wasn't he the one who was studying law?

MISSERIMUS. Yes, maybe he'll defend himself. [*sits down and begins to read*]

MAMACITA. I know his mother. I said a prayer for them too.

DON HERNANDO. Wonderful, wonderful, there's nothing like a prayer.

MISSERIMUS. [*reading*] "*A las cinco de la tarde.*
Eran las cinco en punto de la tarde.
Un nino trajo la blanca sabana
a las cinco de la tarde."

222 THE WONDERFULL YEARE

[*A knock is heard at the door.* MISSERIMUS *keeps reading.* DON HERNANDO *and* MAMACITA *look toward the door.*]

"*Una espuerta de cal ya prevenida a las cinco da la tarde.*"

[*knocking is heard again*]

"*Lo demás era muerta y sólo muerte
a las cinco de la tarde.*"

[*knocking is again heard*]

Well, we had better answer, don't you think?

[DON HERNANDO *goes to door*]

DON HERNANDO.   It's for you, dear, it's Mrs. Sanchez.

[MAMACITA *goes to door.* MRS. SANCHEZ *may be played by one of the two* OLD WOMEN *in the opening of the play, or she may be played as a flirtatious* puta (*whore*).]

MAMACITA.   Ah, Mrs. Sanchez, come in.

MRS. SANCHEZ.   Oh, I just wondered if I could borrow a little sugar. It's so late and all the stores are closed.

MAMACITA.   Certainly. [*goes into kitchen and returns with sugar*] Here you are.

MRS. SANCHEZ.   Oh, thank you so much. Good-bye. Oh, Misserimus, how are you?

MISSERIMUS.   Fine, thank you, Mrs. Sanchez.

MRS. SANCHEZ. Well, good-bye.

MAMACITA. Good-bye.

MISSERIMUS. [*continues reading*]
"*El viento se llevó los algodones,*
a las cinco de la tarde.
Y el exido sembró Cristal y Níquel
a las cinco de la tarde.
Ya luchan la paloma y el leopardo
a las cinco de la tarde.
Y un muslo con un asta desolada
a las cinco de la tarde."

[*Two men enter through the door without knock-*
ing. They wear dark glasses, trench coats and hat.
They are stereotyped detectives. Their arms are
locked together like a dancing team.]

DETECTIVES. [*together*] Come with us, please.

MISSERIMUS. What?

DETECTIVES. You are Misserimus Hidalgo?

MISSERIMUS. Yes, why?

DETECTIVES. Never mind why. Come with us, please.

MAMACITA. He is my son.

DETECTIVES. We are sorry. Come with us.

MISSERIMUS. [*sitting on floor*] Take me.

DON HERNANDO. A man would go on his feet.

MISSERIMUS. Papa, when they come to get you it makes no
difference how you go. I am tired.

DETECTIVES. [*look at each other*] All right.

[*They pick him up and carry him;* UNCLE TÍO *walks out of bathroom.*]

UNCLE. Misserimus.

MISSERIMUS. Yes, Uncle.

[UNCLE *makes the sign of the V for victory;* MISSERIMUS *looks at him incredulously.*]

What?

[*He is carried out.*]

SCENE ELEVEN

[*The two detectives are standing clasping each other's arms.*]

FIRST DETECTIVE. All right, tell them.

SECOND DETECTIVE. Why me?

FIRST DETECTIVE. You went to college.

SECOND DETECTIVE. All right. We had to do it.

FIRST DETECTIVE. Tell them why.

SECOND DETECTIVE. He was a danger.

FIRST DETECTIVE. Give them that Greek bit.

SECOND DETECTIVE. He was a danger to the *polis*. A *polis* can be defined as a city-state, the entirety of which can be traversed in a single day. New York may be described as a *polis*.

FIRST DETECTIVE. They don't look impressed.

SECOND DETECTIVE. He was a big boy now. He had reached the age of responsibility. He was a *virtus*—medieval Latin for manhood.

FIRST DETECTIVE. I didn't like him. I thought he was an uppity spic myself. Show them the map.

[*taking out map, holding it up between them*]

SECOND DETECTIVE. This is New York City. This spot here is Spanish Harlem. The city is in plague now . . .

[*looks at* FIRST DETECTIVE]

Can we tell them that?

FIRST DETECTIVE. It's all right, they can't do anything about it.

SECOND DETECTIVE. Well, the city is in a state of plague. The largest concentration of sewers is right here. We suspect that he was responsible for planning the explosions. Anyway, he knew about it.

FIRST DETECTIVE. Show them the school records.

SECOND DETECTIVE. Yeah, this is the last bit of evidence against him. His high school record says he played hooky no less than forty times in his senior year. And in college he was a rebel.

FIRST DETECTIVE. That's enough.

SECOND DETECTIVE.   Well, anyway, he was a threat.

FIRST DETECTIVE.   Anything else you wanted to say?

SECOND DETECTIVE.   No.

FIRST DETECTIVE.   O.K.

-   [*They look at each other.*]

SECOND DETECTIVE.   Keep defending the faith.

FIRST DETECTIVE.   [*looking at* SECOND DETECTIVE *in astonishment*]
What?

SCENE TWELVE

[MISSERIMUS *walks across stage, wearing same
outfit as in beginning of play. He takes bottle
from pocket and drinks, looks over shoulder. He
snaps fingers and light is thrown on* MAMACITA
and DON HERNANDO. *They do a pantomime of the
usual morning scene. She helps him with his
jacket.* UNCLE TÍO *comes out of the bathroom as
usual and stares at them, then goes off the room.*
MISSERIMUS *snaps fingers again to give them
sound.*]

DON HERNANDO.   Ah, the Catholic school bells are ringing. I
could stand Catholicism for the bells.

MAMACITA.   It's so bad without Misserimus.

DON HERNANDO.   We will not speak of it.

MAMACITA.   Yes, my husband.

> [DON HERNANDO *puts on his coat and makes as if to walk out of door. Stops suddenly, comes back in and kisses* MAMACITA, *then leaves.*]

> [*exit* MAMACITA]

> [MISSERIMUS, *alone on stage again, takes another drink.*]

MISSERIMUS.   You know [*pause*] the human body is such a poor place to have to keep a soul. [*laughs maliciously, looks over his shoulder and exits*]

SCENE THIRTEEN

> [MISSERIMUS *and* MARIA]

MISSERIMUS.   That's all that it's about, honey, that I'm just dying. I'm just falling through the earth, that's all. Like sand.

MARIA.   You're not dying, Misserimus.

MISSERIMUS.   [*crawling about on the floor dramatically*] Yes, I am, I'm dying, I'm dying, everywhere.

MARIA.   Misserimus, get up off that floor.

MISSERIMUS.   Maria, I need some very involved loving.

MARIA. So does everyone.

MISSERIMUS. No, not everyone, just me.

MARIA. That's because you're so self-centered.

MISSERIMUS. Maria, I've decided to marry you.

MARIA. You what?

MISSERIMUS. I've decided to let myself marry you.

MARIA. What . . . why . . . how come?

MISSERIMUS. It will take at least twenty years before the critics understand what I'm doing. I'm going to need someone to help me wait while they catch up.

MARIA. Listen, you want to suffer for your art. I don't want to suffer. I've done enough suffering in this world to last me a lifetime.

MISSERIMUS. My suffering is a lot more interesting than your suffering.

MARIA. Really?

MISSERIMUS. Listen, you knew you had to get me some day.

MARIA. You wouldn't be faithful, anyway.

MISSERIMUS. Why not?

MARIA. You would?

MISSERIMUS. Probably.

MARIA. Would you stop doing all those weird paintings? Of skulls and Madonnas in chains and what not?

MISSERIMUS. That's the way I see, Maria.

MARIA. Well, will you do just a few normal paintings, so that you don't scare people?

MISSERIMUS. [*suddenly very tenderly*] I'd like to paint you.

[MARIA *looks at him.*]

SCENE FOURTEEN

[MISSERIMUS *and* MARIA *are being instructed on the art of packing a suitcase for their honeymoon in Puerto Rico.* CONSUELA *is showing them.* MISSERIMUS *and* MARIA *are seated before her and the open suitcase.*]

CONSUELA. [*acting very much like a salesman*] Now, you'll find that there is a great deal of space which people seldom use.

MISSERIMUS. How interesting.

[MARIA *hits him.*]

MARIA. Misserimus, your sister was nice enough to lend us the luggage for our honeymoon, don't be rude.

MISSERIMUS. Sorry.

CONSUELA. Now then, I find that a lot of things can be put in shoes. Things like stockings and socks, panties and girdles.

MISSERIMUS. She doesn't wear girdles.

MARIA. Shut up!

CONSUELA. And you can put these all inside your shoes, and put them in here. The outer rim of the bag. Then along here, you put your skirts and dresses. And it would also be nice if you put a bar of opened soap inside your suitcase, because I find it gives everything a nice smell. Now it might be a good idea to take a few towels, just in case, you know . . . the hotel might not give you good ones. Now over here you can place your cosmetics and . . .

SCENE FIFTEEN

[MISSERIMUS *and* MARIA *meet the new* LANDLORD.]

LANDLORD. You're the Hidalgos?

MARIA. Yes.

LANDLORD. I'm the new landlord.

MARIA. What happened to Mr. Winters?

LANDLORD. Nothing except he died while you were away on honeymoon.

MISSERIMUS. Oh, sorry to hear that.

LANDLORD. I'm his son.

MISSERIMUS. Oh.

LANDLORD. Now I understand you made some inquiries about the strange odors on the second floor.

MISSERIMUS. No inquiries, complaints.

LANDLORD. Oh, well, that odor is cat piss, the lady downstairs seems to like cats.

MARIA. Urgh.

LANDLORD. I'm sorry, cat urine.

MISSERIMUS. So can't you do anything?

LANDLORD. You should be glad, it keeps the rats away.

MISSERIMUS. Thanks.

LANDLORD. Don't mention it.

[MARIA *looks at* MISSERIMUS.]

SCENE SIXTEEN

[MISSERIMUS' *and* MARIA's *new apartment downtown. They are now neighbors of* CONSUELA *and* ESTEBAN.]

ESTEBAN. Well, here we all are, aren't we?

MARIA. Yes.

CONSUELA. You'll find that it's a nice location down here. The Village isn't far away.

MARIA. Thank you so much for finding us this apartment.

ESTEBAN. I guess we'll be seeing a lot of each other now.

MISSERIMUS. I guess.

ESTEBAN. You know what I was wondering about, Misserimus?

MISSERIMUS. No, Esteban, what were you wondering about?

ESTEBAN. One of your paintings, the one with the motorcycle gang and the Negro guy with the dark glasses.

MISSERIMUS. Oh, you mean *The Fascist State.*

ESTEBAN. Yes, what did you mean in that one?

MISSERIMUS. Oh, the black guy was being executed by the motorcycle gang for listening to music. The motorcycle gang with the helmets and swastikas represent the Fascist State. Pretty simple, no?

ESTEBAN. [*laughing nervously*] Yes, I guess.

SCENE SEVENTEEN

[MISSERIMUS' *and* MARIA's *new apartment. Summertime.*]

MARIA. God, it's so hot in here.

MISERIMUS. [*reading*] Open a window.

MARIA. The windows is open, I mean, the windows are open.

MISSERIMUS. So fan yourself.

> [*He gets up, puts record on record player. John Coltrane's "Impressions of India." The sound comes on offstage, as the scene ends the music is blasting.*]

MARIA. Misserimus, why don't we get an air conditioner?

MISSERIMUS. A what?

MARIA. Will you turn that thing down? An air conditioner. Your sister has one, you know?

MISSERIMUS. So what?

MARIA. You know people don't get air conditioners for status, they get them because they're comfortable.

MISSERIMUS. I'll remember that, people get air conditioners because they are comfortable.

MARIA. We don't have to get a big one, just a nice small inexpensive one.

MISSERIMUS. Really.

MARIA. What difference does it make anyway, I'm the one that's working.

MISSERIMUS. Don't start now, Maria.

MARIA.   "Don't start now, Maria," he says. You get a chance to lecture at the New School. And you turn it down. Do you know how many artists would love a chance to lecture there?

MISSERIMUS.   I don't care. I don't want to lecture anybody on anything.

MARIA.   All right, do what you want to do, but I'm getting an air conditioner.

[*The music—Coltrane's "Impressions"—gets louder as the scene dissolves.*]

SCENE EIGHTEEN

[*The* Para Distinción *Award. A woman,* ROSA MUNDI, *is called up to make the dedication. She may be played by one of the three* OLD WOMEN *in the opening of the play. She is rather stout, middle-aged.* MAMACITA *is seated in the crowd. After receiving award,* MISSERIMUS (*who is dressed in his paint-splattered dungarees and a clean shirt with tie and jacket*) *gives the silver cup to* MAMACITA *to the joyous applause of the onlookers.*]

SPEAKER.   And now, *señors and señoras,* I would like to present to you a truly magnificent artist. A young maestro, the one who *El Diario* has called, "The Puerto Rican Picasso." Our very own Misserimus Hidalgo.

MAMACITA.   That's my son. [*looks about her proudly*]

SPEAKER. It was not that long ago that he was working in my store sweeping up and tending to things, but one could see even then, the talent in his young eyes.

CROWD. Yes, yes.

SPEAKER. He was always a quiet boy . . .

MAMACITA. Yes, always very quiet.

SPEAKER. But, not too quiet.

MAMACITA. No, not too quiet.

SPEAKER. I remember once he drew the face of one of my customers on a box top. [*laughs*] A very good caricature too, but after all, I had to scold him a little. But he's not drawing on box tops anymore. *Que bueno, que bueno.*

And now, to present this award which was obtained by the Puerto Rican merchants' guild, at great expense to everyone involved, [*long pause*] is Señora Rosa Mundi, the wife of Philipe the baker.

[*a large round of applause*]

ROSA MUNDI. [*entering in evening dress and silver high-heeled shoes. She is reading her speech*] *Bienvenido,* my friends. I am very honored tonight to be asked to present to the young Misserimus this award for distinction in the art of painting and culture. I know his family must be very proud as are we all.

The road of the Puerto Rican in this country is a dusty one. [*pause*] It is a dusty road that we travel. From the small tropical stores, to the jobs as superintendents [*stumbles on word*] of buildings. Then further up the ladder to the *bodega* owner and then finally to the owner of funeral homes.

GONZALEZ. [*smiling heartily*] Yes, yes.

ROSA MUNDI. Yes, it is a difficult path. We are not understood by many, and we are not liked by most. We have nothing for comfort but ourselves. We are not black. We are not white.

GONZALEZ. We're not pink either, heh, heh.

[*laughter*]

ROSA MUNDI. [*rereads*] We are not black, we are not white, yet we are a happy people. We are proud of our musicians and artists. For they give to the world outside, the joy of our streets. [*long pause; she looks around for applause*] And so now without further delay, I now present the *Para Distinción* award to Misserimus Hidalgo for . . . um . . . distinction. Misserimus Hidalgo.

[*more applause,* MISSERIMUS *gets award*]

MISSERIMUS. [*seeming shy*] I would like to thank everyone concerned with this. My mother, [*waves*] my father, my priest, the Gonzalez funeral home [*they laugh*] and the New York City Police Department. Heh heh. Without everyone it would not have been possible for me to have my inspiration to paint. [*pause*] You are my art. [*large applause*] Thank you, thank you all. [*Gives the upturned thumb signal. Kisses* ROSA MUNDI *on the cheek and places the award in* MAMACITA's *hand and kisses her too.*]

SCENE NINETEEN

[*The* PRIEST. *A young priest in his thirties, walks across stage alone. He is from Boston and has been in New York for about seven years.*]

PRIEST.   And would you not then say, Malachi, that in this instance the church is the sole refuge of the disinherited masses of the world? [*pause*] What is the church's stand on the issue of pestilence and plague? I think more truthfully the question might be asked, what has the church to do with the concerns of the city. The answer is, nothing.

We have nothing to do with the ephemeral modalities which the city experiences. The city, even the most modern of cities, is but a halfway house in the midst of temporal pilgrimage. We cannot speak of matters of sin or pain, but only of privations.

When I first came to this place, I had certain ideas, certain concepts. I had come from Boston. The Archdiocese saw fit to place me in this bondage, [*pause*] in this situation, of being in charge of a wholly Spanish parish. They were not overly interested in Thomas Aquinas, or for that matter in the writings of Juan De la Cruz, Saint John of the Cross.

It was very difficult for me to arrive at any sort of prehension as to what exactly these people were about. The nature of their faith is far more immediate and actual than any I had heretofore encountered.

I first had to understand that nothing in their history had been lost. I know this sounds absurd at first hearing it, but it's true. Everything which has gone before: the Moors, the Spanish, the Indian, has all been, how shall I say, hidden but yet present.

I walk out into these streets and find myself confronting over two thousand years. And it's sometimes very frightening. I am the parish father, I have to keep within my consciousness the details of each family, their peculiarities, a record of their offenses, births, deaths, etc.

As regards the plague, [*pause*] I cannot speak of it with any of the parishioners. We, in our role as God's advocate, may only on occasions of distress manifest a sort of outward visible sign which bespeaks an inward spiritual grace. The church's answer to all crises, be they famine, pestilence, war or any other of the apocalyptical riders, is and has been: birth. Procreation outlives everything. And these are, goodness knows, a fecund people. And this in the final analysis will see us right.

SCENE TWENTY

[*A cemetery.* MISSERIMUS' *mother's funeral. It is winter. Everyone has their coats on as they stand about coffin. They are waiting for the priest who is forty-five minutes late. Finally* GONZALEZ *the funeral director decides to perform the ceremony. At the conclusion of the scene, the coffin is pulled (by the two* DETECTIVES*) by two ropes to the back of the stage, symbolizing the lowering of the coffin. On the coffin is printed the word:* COFFIN.]

GONZALEZ. Well, we've waited forty-five minutes and the priest still hasn't gotten here.

TOMASIO. Hey, I'm very sorry, Misserimus, your mother was a very beautiful person.

MISSERIMUS. Thank you very much for coming, Tomasio, it means a lot to me to see you.

TOMASIO. Your paintings have changed a lot, Misserimus. I never thought I'd see you doing still lifes and portrait painting.

MISSERIMUS. One changes, friend, you get older, you change.

TOMASIO. Have your critics had anything to do with it?

MISSERIMUS. No, critics get old, painters get old, everybody gets old and then they die. I just feel different these days, that's all.

CONSUELA. What was it that Mother died of, Papacito?

DON HERNANDO. I don't know really, it was so fast.

ESTEBAN. She died of the vapors.

GONZALEZ. Yes, I think you're right, Esteban, it said something about a vapor of the brain on her death certificate.

ESTEBAN. Yes, it was the vapors, you can tell by the swelling in the face.

GONZALEZ. Well, it seems as though the priest got lost so if no one objects I'll do the ceremony.

DON HERNANDO. All right, Gonzalez.

GONZALEZ. [*taking off hat*] When we are on the earth we walk
  upright,
when we die we lie down.
The Lord giveth and then we get tired.
Blessed be the name of the Lord.

                                        Amen.

CONSUELA. [*tearfully*] Mamacita, Mamacita.

GONZALEZ. You may deposit flowers.

  [*They throw flowers on the coffin as it is being
  pulled away.*]

  Please, sign the book of visitors so that we may send
  thank-you cards.

  [*The* TWO WOMEN *of the first scene approach*
  DON HERNANDO.]

FIRST OLD WOMAN. Don Hernando, we are very sorry for your
  grief.

DON HERNANDO. Thank you all, very much.

SECOND OLD WOMAN. You must be feeling great pain.

DON HERNANDO. I don't feel anything yet, it all happened so fast.

FIRST OLD WOMAN. Don Hernando, we hate to bother you at a
  time like this, but you are the only wise person we know.

SECOND OLD WOMAN. Yes, Don Hernando is very wise.

FIRST OLD WOMAN. What we would like is for you to help us
  with our Medicaid papers, we don't understand how to
  go about filing them.

SECOND OLD WOMAN. Yes, you don't have to do it today, but sometime when you have a chance, say, tomorrow or the day after.

DON HERNANDO. Yes, certainly, do you have all of your forms?

SECOND OLD WOMAN. Yes, we have everything.

DON HERNANDO. Then come by my house tomorrow evening.

FIRST OLD WOMAN, SECOND OLD WOMAN. [*together*] Oh thank you, very much.

UNCLE TÍO. [*To* DON HERNANDO] Well, I guess it's just us now, Don Hernando. We'll play cards, or dominoes perhaps.

DON HERNANDO. Yes, Uncle Tío, we'll play a lot now.

[*They walk off together.*]

SCENE TWENTY-ONE

[MISSERIMUS *and* MARIA. MARIA *is dressed in nightgown.*]

MARIA. Aren't you coming to bed?

MISSERIMUS. [*smiling*] Soon, honey, soon.

MARIA. What are you going to do? It's too late to paint. There's no light.

MISSERIMUS. I'm just thinking for a while.

MARIA. Why are you smiling like that? You know you always disturb me when you come in at night. I have to get up to go to work while you stay home and wait for inspiration.

MISSERIMUS. I have to think, honey, that's what my work is about. Everything moves, changes . . . you know? I have to catch those moments of change.

[MARIA *shakes her head in confusion.*]

It's such a funny time now. You don't see it, do you?

MARIA. When I was living uptown all I could see was the bars on the windows. The place was like a prison, everyone looking out from behind their gates. And you would never have moved if I didn't insist.

MISSERIMUS. It's a very funny time. People are beginning to see after all this time that we were right. Guys who worked themselves into nervous wrecks, trying to get into the universities, getting the degrees. Selling their mothers, or themselves, for the papers. And now look at them, [*shows her newspaper*] climbing out of windows, terrified. It's funny.

MARIA. What's funny?

MISSERIMUS. It's the last days and there's no place in the world to hide.

MARIA. I was talking with Roberta today. Do you know what her brother does?

MISSERIMUS. What?

MARIA. He's a rodent eradicator.

MISSERIMUS.   You mean a rat catcher.

MARIA.   He makes good money, you know with what's going on in the city with the plague and everything. [*pause*] You wouldn't have to do it steady or anything.

MISSERIMUS.   Forget it, baby.

MARIA.   Just until you get that gallery exhibit. You could . . .

MISSERIMUS.   Ha ha. [*reaches under her nightgown to undress her*]

MARIA.   Misserimus, no. [*pushes him away and leaves*]

MISSERIMUS.   [*laughing*] What's this, a pussy strike? The last days of the city and absolutely no place to hide.

SCENE TWENTY-TWO

[MISSERIMUS *is teaching at the New School. He lectures to audience as if they were the students.*]

MISSERIMUS.   [*in suit*] And so, students and fellow artists, we see that in El Greco's "The View and Plan of Toledo," Mr. Stein, please, stop picking your nose, it's distracting, we find the perfect union of the mystic and the artist. El Greco gives us a cosmic picture of the city by showing it from two perfectly opposite perspectives. The details of the inhabitants from one and the overall position of the world and the human condition on the other. It is I believe one of the finest paintings ever made. It is the only perfectly Spanish painting. The *cante hondo,* or deep song, can be felt throughout, in the repetition of the images and motifs. That will be all for today, on our next and final meeting we will be discussing Goya's "The Sleep of Reason." Thank you.

SCENE
TWENTY-THREE

[*The whole cast walks across stage led by* MARIA *who is wheeling a baby carriage with the sign* BABY *printed on its side. She is followed by* MIS-SERIMUS, *carrying a blank canvas,* DOÑA MUERTE, ESTEBAN, GONZALEZ, *smiling, preceding a coffin, held by the two* DETECTIVES. *Finally,* DON HER-NANDO *comes out in his white suit, looks at all of them and at the audience.*]

DON HERNANDO.   It was the flowery season of the year.
The tenement houses are making love to the sky.